P9-BYQ-195

# 54

Written by Gary Lawrence Pesso

Edited by Cassidy Paige Warner

Cover design by Oliver Graham Pesso

*For Tracy, Oliver and Chloe*

All rights reserved. No part of this publication may be reproduced in any form or by any electronic or mechanical means, including information storage or retrieval devices or systems, without prior written permission of Gary L. Pesso. Any unauthorized use, distribution or reproduction of this book is illegal and it is protected by the copyright laws of The United States of America and cooperating Countries.

Copyright 2010 Case # 1-509875541
Registration # TXu 1-724-982
ISBN-13: 9781682739068
Published 2016 – Printed in the USA

Driving Range / Practice Green
Warm-Ups


If you've never spent a fall day in New England, you need to put it on your Bucket List. The scenery, the weather, and the golf are beyond amazing on a mid-October day. Today is the Fall Classic at Maple Ridge Golf Course, one of the best public golf courses in New England which is located just north of Boston and the conditions couldn't be more perfect. Temperatures are in the mid-sixties, orange and red leaves dominate the landscape as far as the eye can see, there's hardly a cloud in the sky, and a slight wind blows from the east. I couldn't ask for a better day to spend playing golf.

Today's event is a great tournament that brings out the top local golfers and attracts many of the teaching pros from New England. The entry fee is a stiff $500 per player which weeds out many of the undesirables and makes it as serious a tournament as you can get outside the professional tours. The event is open to pros but most players are local amateurs like me who may have some collegiate golf experience. I've played in this tournament each of the first four years of its existence and I generally do well, though I have never finished higher than fifth.

My best friend and golf buddy Max Johnson is playing in it like he always does but for the first time and by the luck of the draw, we're paired together, just like the days when we were at the University of North Carolina. Normally we're drawn into different groups to run through the course so this will be a special treat. He usually flies in a day or two early so we can get in a practice round and catch up on each other's lives but this year he arrived late after meeting with a major golf distributor in New York. He got in last night and stayed out by Logan Airport so he didn't have to drive the extra distance to my place.

The last time we saw each other was a year ago at this same event and this has been the longest stretch we've ever been separated since befriending one another. Although we live over two thousand miles apart, we usually find the time to get together and play golf at least a couple of times a year. This year has been especially chaotic for both of us and we somehow didn't manage to find the time. I first see Max this morning as I get to the driving range where he is already there hitting balls.

I stroll up behind him so that he can't see me and ask, "You expect to beat me with that ugly-looking swing?"

He turns around and gives me a giant bear hug. "How the hell did you make it so we can play together? Did you pay off Joey?" He lets out a bark of infectious laughter, and I join in.

It's great to see Max. He's the brother I never had and we've been thick as thieves since we first met nearly fourteen years ago. Though we are itching to recount the latest and greatest in our lives—and trust me, there is a lot we have to discuss—our starting time is in less than thirty minutes and we both need to get warmed up.

"Don't worry about it, we have all day to talk. See you on the first tee." I turn to walk over to the sand trap and my eye is caught by the young kid hitting balls next to Max. I hadn't noticed him when I first came over, but as I take a closer look, I realize this kid can't be older than fourteen, if that. As I watch him hit a few balls, I immediately see what a wonderful swing he has. I stand there for a moment, get Max's attention, and motion to the young man.

Max walks behind him to get next to me and whispers in my ear, "I've watched this kid since I got here, and I haven't seen him hit a bad shot yet."

The kid turns to us, looking a little annoyed that we're watching him. I'm just about to say something reassuring when the head pro at the club puts his hand on my shoulder. "Colby, come here," he says to the kid, "I want to introduce you to two of the better players in the field with you today."

I give Joey a disbelieving look. There's no way this kid is playing in

4

the tournament. But as I eye him up, I'm reminded that Joey Henderson never says anything he doesn't mean. He's an older guy who has been the pro here for ages and he single-handedly runs this tournament. He played in a handful of PGA events in the early 1970's and he can scout out talent faster than any pro I know.

Colby looks less aggravated and comes over to us. "Colby Kittleson, meet Jim Peters and Max Johnson." We shake hands with the young protégé as Joey tells us that he's been working with him for a few months. "He's a scratch golfer and will turn fourteen next month. And boys, you better watch out for this kid; he's the real deal and he has as good a chance as anyone to win out here today."

*Really?* I think to myself. He's still thirteen and must play the same back tees like the rest of us. He shakes our hands maturely enough and says, "It's nice to meet you."

As he goes back to hitting balls, I realize Joey might be right. Colby pulls his driver and proceeds to hit a series of shots with the precision of a pro. His distance is a touch short compared to some of the long hitters out here but he looks to have enough game to be competitive out here today, anyway.

"Good luck, Colby, hit 'em well today," I tell him, and then go to the sand trap to get ready. Max heads back to his spot on the range to clobber a few more practice shots.

Joey stops on his way to greet the players teeing off on the first hole and adds one more thing. "The kid's playing in front of you today, so you're in for a treat if you get to see him manage his way around the course. Good luck, Jim."

I nod my acknowledgement and get back to focusing on the balls in the bunker. I find warming up in the sand helps me get some feel before cranking out shots on the range. It's a routine both Max and I worked out in college. For a tournament like this, I usually like at least forty-five minutes to practice; but

I've been so busy lately that getting here with half an hour to spare was the best I could do.

I glance over at Max. Since he has worked his way up to his driver, he has been here for at least twenty minutes already. We have so much in common when it comes to golf, I know he has already hit his sand shots and worked through the rest of his golf bag. He'll work on that for a few more minutes, and then it's over to the practice green to spend the rest of his time hitting a variety of putts before we tee off. I'll have to shorten my normal routine to get in as much as I can, but I'm not too worried. I've had a lot on my mind lately and just being out here for the next four-and-a-half hours with Max is going to be great, no matter how I play.

Hole #1

Par 5 – 525 yards

I have a thorough-but-quick warm up, Max and I walk toward the first tee just in time to see Colby hit one right down the middle of the fairway. I'm amazed at how far he drives his ball, but it doesn't really surprise me too much. With the way the junior tours have progressed since Tiger Woods came along, kids today already have a ton of tournament experience by the time they reach Colby's age, and he's obviously been at this awhile if he's playing at this level. Joey winks at me as the kid walks off the tee. He is deservingly proud of his student and it wouldn't surprise me if Joey fronted the money for Colby to play today.

The third member of our group joins us as we step onto the tee and introduces himself. Dustin Craft is a twenty-three-year-old assistant pro from Providence who has just finished college and is working towards his "Class A" pro status on his way to being a head pro someday. He hails from Oklahoma, went through the Golf Academy of America in Orlando and my initial impression is he has some skills as I saw him hit a few shots on the range. It should be fun watching him play today.

The threesome format used in this tournament keeps the game moving at a steady pace and makes for a fun round of golf. It is a one-day, eighteen-hole stroke-play event where the lowest score wins and ties for first go to a sudden death playoff, which happened in two of the four tournaments to date. The lowest winning score has been a sixty-five.

As far as tournaments go, this one isn't our first. Max and I played number one and two on our college team, respectively, and it took a lot of work to get there. Max's father was a teaching pro in Southern California, where Max grew up. He has more talent than anyone I know and in college I was convinced he would make it onto the professional tour someday. But his biggest problem is that he can't seem to keep his head in the game. Max always finds a way to sabotage a good run and let his temper get the best of him. I don't have his ball-striking ability, but I have always been a better putter and, unlike him, I can handle pressure when it counts.

Joey meets us on the first tee to hand out score cards and review the rules of the day, breaking me from my reminiscing. Spectators are allowed to follow along, but this isn't a big enough event to draw any serious crowds aside from the local newspaper reporters and an occasional TV crew who cover the event, since it raises money for local charities. Today, there are a handful of people watching the group ahead of us. As far as I can tell, it is Colby's parents and a few other relatives and friends. I watch them head down the fairway and make a point to look up in time to see the kid hit his second shot. From the tee, it looks like he's still a long way to the green, it appears he hits a fairway wood and I'll be damned if he didn't make it just short of the green. A damn impressive feat for anyone, and especially for someone his age.

I take a moment to focus and scan the first hole. It is a straight-ahead par five with the green reachable in two if you hit the fairway on the drive. I always like starting on a hole I have a good chance to birdie, since, as my college coach always used to say, "You can't birdie them all unless you birdie the first!"

Joey snaps me out of my reverie as he announces us one by one. First up is Dustin. He hits it long, but pushes it off into the right-hand rough. It's not a bad shot, but it will be difficult to reach the green from the rough on the next shot. I'm up next, and I manage to pipe one down the middle. Max follows with an almost identical drive. We're off!

As we pick up our bags and head off the tee box, Max puts his hand on my shoulder and says, "So, who's this new girl you're hanging out with?" He doesn't have any idea of whether or not there is someone, but it's his way of saying, "Let's get started."

When Max and I reported to college our freshman year, we both had full golf scholarships and were expected to be the future of the team. They already had a good organization, but four of their top players graduated the previous year and they were looking to us to be part of their rebuilding process.

The head coach, Jack Stone, was not only a great golf coach, but also a great friend. We still stay in close contact, even today. Jack constantly reminded us that golf is a game and it should be played for fun, otherwise it isn't worth playing. He was the reason I picked North Carolina over the other offers I had.

Max's father was instrumental in getting Max there. He had taught Max everything he could about playing golf, but somewhere along the line, he had missed teaching his son to control his temper. Therefore, he believed a guy like Jack Stone could help Max's mental approach to the game.

Max and I met at orientation about a month before school started. We instantly liked each other, and after playing our first round together that weekend, we arranged to be roommates in the freshman dorm. Jack liked the way Max and I formed this early bond, and he played off it. He taught us how to maximize our potential, and we immediately used this knowledge to take advantage of numerous opportunities to hustle other golfers at the local courses. I don't think that was what Jack had in mind, but it was a great way for us to make some extra cash.

As much as Jack had us focus on our mental attitude when playing golf, when it came to competition, he wanted us to be on cruise control. The goal was to not over think the game, but to find something to take our minds off the intense competition and let our bodies do what they had been trained to do. He felt too many golfers dwell on their mistakes and let their minds take them out of the game. "You're going to make many mistakes throughout every eighteen holes you play," he would always tell us. "It's not about the mistakes, it's about how you handle those mistakes and turn bad shots into opportunities to make great recoveries." Jack taught us that thinking of something else during competition allowed your mind to be at ease and gives your body the ability to hit every shot with your greatest potential. By the time you're playing at the collegiate level, you should already know how to hit the variety of golf shots necessary to score under par. It's your mind that screws it up. For Max and me, finding that "something else" to think about was easy; all we had to do was talk about girls.

***

As we reach our drives, we're engaged in a conversation about this girl Max has been spending time with. Her name is Vanessa and she's a twenty-seven-year-old sales rep for a medical company in Phoenix, very close to where Max lives. He moved there a few years after college and took a job with Ping, a major golf club company, which allows him to travel the pro golf tours and stay involved in the game he loves. Although Max won many college golf tournaments, the pro tour was just too far out of reach; but he has been able to turn his skills into a nice living. Vanessa is the first girl I've ever heard Max seem so seriously interested in. I'm surprised this is the first I've heard of her, but the past year has been so crazy, I suppose we haven't had much time to talk.

While we wait for the players in front of us to reach the green, I see Colby prepare to hit his third shot. He has a short pitch to the flag, and when the group following him lets out a loud roar, I realize he's eagled the first hole. Without being overly greedy, my plan is doing my best to make a birdie on this reachable par 5, and it dawns on me if I do, I'll already be a stroke down to a thirteen-year-old.

Dustin is first to hit his second shot. He has to lay-up short of the green

10

from the thick rough, and he does so without any problem. I am next with 243 yards to the pin, straight ahead with the only obstacle being a greenside bunker short and left of the green. The shot is setup well for a slight fade from the left, and I hit a three wood just inside the bunker to the front edge of the green. Max is 15 yards ahead of me, also in the fairway, and he hits a hybrid safely onto the green with a good chance for eagle. He turns to continue telling me about his latest "lady" as we start making our way farther up the hole.

***

Vanessa was on the driving range at a public golf course in Phoenix when Max first saw her. She was a real beginner and easy prey for a seasoned veteran like Max. He positioned himself behind her so he could keep an eye on here and completely check her out in the process. Max is great at explaining women in detail, and by the time he was done describing her—including her perfect little butt, which he was completely in awe of, standing behind her that first day—I could practically see her myself. It wasn't long before she got frustrated trying to hit the little ball, which gave Max the perfect opportunity to make his move. He offered to help her with her swing. It was too simple; she was taken by his knowledge of the game, good looks, and easy-going attitude. I always wished that was the guy who would show up on the tee instead of the intense Max who could throw a club as far as most people can hit a driver.

He met Vanessa directly after she had broken up with her boyfriend. She claimed she couldn't imagine getting into another relationship, but Max knew she was secretly falling for him. It turned out that her ex-boyfriend had hit her a few times when he had been drinking, and it took her a while to figure out she was in an abusive relationship. He was apparently terrific to her when he was sober, and she wanted to believe it wasn't a pattern. But after it happened a few times, she dumped him. They were together over a year before he hit her,

11

so she thought for sure she knew him, but as time went on, it proved too difficult to believe him any longer and she was smart enough to get out. Vanessa had decided to take up golf purely to spite him, since he told her she would never be able to handle the sport. To prove him wrong, she had trekked out to the range that day. She had sworn to herself she would never talk to the loser again, so learning to play golf was more about proving to herself that her ex was a jerk.

*** 

Dustin steps up for his third shot. He has 50 yards straight at the flag and hits a lob wedge tight to the pin, but his ball spins back hard to leave him with a 20-foot birdie putt. I have a long 60-plus-foot putt for eagle, which I manage to snuggle up to just about three feet from the pin. Max is next with 35 feet and a slight downhill left-to-right breaking putt. He nearly holes it, taps in for birdie, and cracks a huge smile. Dustin, too, comes close, but he has to settle for par. I easily make my short putt for my first birdie of the day. Max and I bump knuckles like we've done a million times before and almost simultaneously say, "The 54 watch is on!"

Hole #2

Par 4 – 412 yards

The "54 watch" is what our coach Jack always talked about. He would say, "You can never be fully satisfied with a round of golf until you birdie every hole and shoot 54." It has never been done, and there have only been a few sub-60 rounds ever recorded on all the golf tours in the world. The original Mr. 59 was Al Geiberger, who was the first to ever shoot that number in a PGA tour event. There have recently been a few scores lower than 59 in other golf outings, but 54 has only been a fantasy. And Jack believed it could be done.

I have the honors of driving first on the next hole, and as I look up ahead, Colby's group is already out of range, approaching the green. Suddenly a feeling of competitiveness starts pumping through my veins. "I'm going to have to play lights-out just to stand a chance against this kid. Luckily, I comfortably hit a smooth one up the right side of the fairway, leaving a short iron into a slightly elevated green. Max hits a hard three wood very close to my drive, and Dustin pipes a driver 20 yards past us in the fairway. He doesn't seem very pleased with our birdies, nor about how good Max and I are getting along. He appears to have what we call a little "red ass" in his shot—that is, he is rather upset with making a par on the first hole and is really going after this tee shot.

Maple Ridge as a course leaves a lot of opportunities for birdies, even from the back tees we're required to hit from during this tournament. I've always made a fair number of birdies here, but unfortunately, I've also had my share of bogies.

"So, how often are you seeing this Vanessa girl?" I ask.

Max grins slightly. "Oh, you know, whenever I get a chance." He lets that hang as he does his normal pre-shot routine, complete with a couple practice swings and stance-modifying. He is first to hit the second shot, he has 159 yards and a little uphill to a green with two sand bunkers behind it. There is a slight tail wind, and he tries to feather in a smooth seven iron. But just as he hits, the wind dies, his ball lands on the front edge of the green and rolls back down the hill a few yards, leaving him with a relatively easy chip to the pin.

I have 152 yards left—a similar shot—and choose hitting a full 8 iron. I hit it absolutely perfect. We can't see it from where we stand, but two people who are following Dustin have walked up ahead and are watching from behind the green. When they start clapping, I know it has to be close.

I put the club back in my bag and ask, "So she's a redhead, huh?"

Max smiles. "Yeah, she's not my typical type, right?" He seems to have read my mind. I've never seen him go for a redhead before. We fall silent again as our playing partner prepares for his second shot on the hole.

Dustin has less than 135 yards to the pin and he works his ball to the middle of the green. The pin is located deep towards the back of the green, and we can see he isn't happy with the shot. Kids today expect so much from their game, and I think Dustin puts a lot of pressure on himself to play well. He seems like a nice guy, but I'm sure he feels like the third wheel around us. I'm not normally paired with anyone I'm as close to as Max for this event, so I usually have my game face on and don't do a lot of talking.

But today is different.

Very different.

It turns out the two-people watching Dustin are his parents. They stay far ahead of us at all times so as not to disturb their son "at work." It doesn't bother me to have spectators. In fact, I enjoy it. In college, we played a lot of tournaments with people hanging around. This tournament today is nothing like the pro tour, but there is usually enough of an audience to invoke memories of the first time playing for a crowd. There's a local radio celebrity playing a few groups ahead of us, and although he's a decent player, he draws spectators more on the antics from his radio show than his golf talent. I played with him four years ago in this event and it was more like a circus show as the day went on and

14

he was out of contention. It was distracting, but I tried my best to stay out of his way and play my game. I finished twelfth that year, shooting two over par. Usually, something around 67 wins this event; there are some excellent golfers in this area.

When we get up to Max's ball, we can finally see mine sitting less than two feet from the cup. I figured it was close, but this is more than I had hoped for. They both easily manage their shots for tap-in pars, while I drop in my second birdie in as many holes. Max gives me another fist-full of knuckles while Dustin nods his approval in my direction. However, being two strokes behind me isn't sitting well with him, and we don't have much conversation together. He is intently focused on his game while Max and I are still getting caught up.

Hole #3

Par 4 – 339 yards

Every good golf course should have a reachable par 4 that you can take a run at, and this is it. I've always liked playing on courses with a hole like this, and today they have it set up with a front pin, which will make it even easier to reach from the tee. They allow us to use range finders in this event. The technology has become so popular that everyone has one these days, and since they don't allow you to have a caddy for the tournament, the range finder keeps up the pace-of-play by giving the exact yardage of every shot. The hole is playing 322 yards today, which is reachable with a big drive. As an illustration of this, the group ahead of us is already out of sight. I wonder if Colby made birdie here and if he's three or four under par through the first three holes. I'm glad his group has pulled out of sight and I remind myself to forget about him and play my own game.

Overall, it's a straight-forward hole. Two small bunkers frame the front of the green, but there is a gap to shoot between if you hit the ball just right. If you're slightly off-line, it usually gets caught in one of the bunkers. I am able to hit a slight fade off of the left-hand bunker and roll it onto the green. My ball comes in hot and rolls toward the back, but stays safely on the green. Max has a very similar shot, but catches the right edge of the left bunker. He'll have an easy shot from there, especially because his sand game has always been one of his strengths. His father used to have him hit garbage pail-sized buckets of balls from the sand every day, even before school a few days a week, since Max enjoyed it when he was young. He only hated picking up the balls afterwards. Dustin hits third and gets a little wild in his swing. His ball goes a long way, but off-line left, and he'll have a very difficult up-and-down shot from the deeper rough.

Max goes on to tell me about Vanessa's quirky attitude as we step off the tee and start making our way down the fairway.

"She has this great smile, and she makes me laugh."

"She makes you laugh?"

He chuckles lightly. "Yeah, every time I'm around her." Max grins slightly, looking out toward the pin.

In all the years I've known him, he's never once told me about a girl's personality. There must be something much more serious going on here than he was initially leading me to believe. I have always been more of a romantic than Max, and as much as I loved chasing women with him in college, I tended to have more "relationships" while he preferred one-night stands. Usually in eighteen holes, he can tell me stories of a dozen different women in the few months we generally have between visits. However, here we are approaching the third green, and all I've heard about is Vanessa. I can tell this round is only going to be about one girl for Max. Most of the girls he speaks of don't have names beyond the description, "Last night, this chick named Beth or Betty or Barbie was incredible!"

"So, what's Vanessa like?"

"Well, we took a trip this summer to Southern California…"

***

The trip was for a PGA tour event that Max had to be at. He goes to many such events throughout the year as a liaison for Ping and the tour players, bringing the latest technology for players to try. He loves golf, and being there in this capacity is very good for him. He gave up his hopes of being a tour player after college, since the stress of serious competition was too much for him, so this job is a great way to keep him in the thick of things in the golf world. Max makes a good living and has great benefits, such as being able to travel all over with the company, including attending his favorite event, the

17

British Open.

On this trip to California, Max was able to bring Vanessa using free travel miles. He upgraded his room to a suite at a fancy hotel south of LA, and they arrived the Saturday before the tour event. Max would usually show up on Tuesday morning of the tour stops and hang around until late Wednesday, when the players would finish up their practice rounds. There wasn't much for him to do once the event started, so all his contact was during the two days prior to the start of the competition. That week, he brought Vanessa out for the weekend to spend a few days relaxing with her at the pool and dining out.

\*\*\*

"Have you ever spent more than one night in a hotel with the same woman before?" I ask, mildly surprised.

"Not that I can recall." Max smirks.

This really *is* more serious than I had imagined!

\*\*\*

They were lying out by the pool at their hotel, having a few drinks and getting along well. Their room was just off the pool, so they could easily go in and out during the day for the numerous lovemaking sessions. It was late afternoon when they popped inside for another bout. Max told me Vanessa was the first girl he ever met who could keep up with him sexually. Since this was their second time today, there was a lot more foreplay, and he thoroughly enjoyed learning every inch of her magnificent body. She was a good athlete and worked out regularly, which left her with what Max referred to as "the kind of body you could spend a week examining and never find a flaw." Vanessa was very adventurous, though Max was very clear about what a "nice" girl she was. Although her experiences had only been with a few different men in her life, she was very excitable and willing to experiment with Max, which he greatly appreciated.

At this point, they were enthralled in one of the most incredible sexual encounters of his life. They were an hour into it, Vanessa was on top, and their bodies were moving together in perfect unison. Both were about to reach the pinnacle of the afternoon when the building suddenly began to tremble. A small and quick earthquake had made the hotel shake just enough to disturb their moment. Max wasn't sure what happened at first, but then he could actually see the walls of their hotel room start to wiggle. He realized through his half-dazed state that it wasn't their love-making causing it and he shouted, "Earthquake!"

Vanessa had never experienced an earthquake before, and she did not handle it well. She jumped straight off him and cleared the end of the bed in one motion. She screamed and ran for the door.

\*\*\*

Max needs to stop talking as we reach the bunker where his ball has settled. Dustin finds his ball and makes an incredible shot to the pin, leaving a very makeable birdie. I am so engrossed in this story, I don't pay much attention to Dustin's shot, but we are conscious enough to lower our voices while he hits. Max is now in the bunker, making his pre-shot waggle, and keeps talking. He pauses for a quick moment, swings down and through with the precision of a tour player, and his ball stops eight feet from the pin. Max only watches the ball briefly before continuing with his story about the earthquake.

\*\*\*

The room was still shaking. He had been in tremors before, but this

19

was particularly intense. By the time Vanessa hit the door, the shaking had almost stopped; but she kept on going.

Once he got to the door, Vanessa was outside by the pool—stark naked and looking like the world was coming to an end. Since the quake was already over, Max was pulling on a robe and making for the door. His eyes were glued to Vanessa, who was looking up at the building with terror in her eyes. It was obvious she was oblivious to the fact she was outside in front of a hotel-full of strangers without anything on. In her defense, most people at the pool were up out of their chairs and somewhat panicked themselves, but most had caught more than an eyeful of Vanessa. Max was tying his robe while heading out to rescue her from this ground shaking experience. On his way out the door to bring her back inside he couldn't help but notice how beautiful she was there, her long red hair cascading over her small and athletic body, her breasts perfect in the sunshine. As much as he wanted to just stare at her, he didn't want to leave her out there naked in front of everyone. Despite being terrified, she was stunning. She was breathing heavily like she had just run a marathon, and the sweat on her body was glistening as the afternoon sun was setting.

***

I am now over my putt and need to concentrate for a moment, so he stops while I take my shot. It is for an eagle from about 50 feet away, slightly downhill, and pretty straight. I leave it a good five feet short. As I mark my ball, Max tells me how he ran out to bring her back into their room.

***

She was shaking and very confused, with no idea how she got outside, naked, with everyone staring at her. He wrapped her in her own bathrobe and coaxed her back to the room and calmed her down. It took her a few minutes to realize what had happened. And then the embarrassment kicked in and she giggled nervously, completely out of control, for quite some time. It took her the rest of the day to stop blushing.

***

Max stands over his putt with this huge smile, looks down, and smoothly strokes the ball toward the hole. He misses it by inches, taps it in from the other side, and I think for sure the putter is about to go flying across the green as I've seen him do so many times in the past after missing an opportunity for an easy birdie. However, he looks up at me and says frankly, "It was the most memorable sexual moment of my life."

Wow, this is surely a different Max. He has an inner peace about him while he talks about Vanessa, and it is infectious to be with him. Dustin knocks in his putt and I follow. It was a great three for Dustin, and he is pumped about picking up a stroke. Mine seems almost routine, and I look to Max for more of this story.

***

They stayed in the room the rest of the weekend, only going outside on occasion to get some sun or find something other than room service to eat. To my utter disbelief, it's obvious that he was falling in love with her.

Hole #4

Par 3 – 154 yards

As we walk to the next hole, I write down my score and realize I have started this round three under par for the first three holes and hadn't realized it. The memory of a similar situation in college immediately forces its way to the forefront of my mind. I *can't* let myself make the same mistake today.

\*\*\*

It was ten years ago. I was 22, a senior in college, and Max and I were playing in a tournament in Tennessee. I had been up the entire night before with a girl I had literally run into. She was young and beautiful, and I was crazy about her. We hung out together all night, reluctant to part even as the sun was rising. I barely had enough time to get to my hotel room, grab my equipment, and head to the golf course. Max gave me a devilish smile as we left for the course and said, "She better have been good. Today is a big tournament."

When we arrived at the course, our coach wasn't very pleased with my disheveled appearance and monstrous bags under my eyes. He reminded me why we were there, and I felt like I had already let him down before taking my first swing.

Max and I started in on reliving my night the moment our feet touched the driving range. I couldn't stop talking about Samantha--or Sammy, as she preferred. I had met my parents at Vito's Italian restaurant in Memphis for an early dinner, since they were doing a road trip across the country and timed it to meet me for a meal as they passed through. Afterward, I walked them to their car and said goodbye. As I walked back toward my hotel, I rounded a corner and literally crashed into this beautiful young lady, knocking her to the ground. Call it fate, or just plain inattention. We both came around the corner, not watching where we were going, and being smaller than I am, she took the brunt of the collision. I thought I had hurt her badly, since it sounded like she was crying softly. She had her head down, and her long brown hair was covering her face. I could see blood dripping onto one of her magnificent legs, which were folded under her like a pretzel. Although, I couldn't see her face from my vantage point above her, she was incredibly sexy looking. She was wearing a tight t-shirt which showed off her breasts, and a mini skirt that wasn't covering very much of her tangled body below me. Even though I was seriously concerned about what I had done to her, I was praying her face looked as good as the rest of her.

I finally bent down and, as sincerely as I have ever been, asked, "Are you okay?" I started to reach out to help her, but something kept me from touching her. Perhaps it was simply her perfection.

She looked up, and I could see blood coming from her lower lip. There wasn't a lot of it, but it confirmed my notion that I had hurt her. However, as she raised her head to look at me, it quickly became apparent that her sobs weren't sobs at all. She was laughing, and now even louder than before. Despite the trickle of blood on her lip, she was remarkably beautiful. I couldn't stop staring at her.

She wiped away a tear of mirth and said, "I'm so sorry! I should have been paying more attention." She pushed herself to her feet and gave me an embarrassed smile as she started smoothing out her rumpled clothes.

I had a nervous feeling of relief and tried to get a grip on what just happened. She giggled and tried to apologize again. I interrupted her and said, "No, it was my fault. I'm so sorry I knocked you down."

Neither of us had anything to wipe away the blood, but there was a little store open across the street. I told her to wait there as I dashed over to the store. The clerk had seen what happened and helpfully gave me some paper towels and tissues.

"Thank you," she said as I returned to help her. "By the way, my name's Sammy."

I smiled nervously. "I'm Jim. Sorry again for running into you."

"You really don't have to worry about it." This pronouncement was followed by a distinctly awkward pause. I had no idea how to move forward, but Sammy saved it. "I'm feeling a little light-headed and need to sit down."

We relocated to some steps nearby, and I asked her again if she was alright. She assured me she was, she just needed a minute. The laughter had stopped and I could tell she was feeling the pain in her lip. I felt incredibly guilty, but not necessarily because of the injury I had caused. Rather, I was so happy this had happened, even though I knew she had received the worse end of the deal. I don't know if I believe in love-at-first-sight, but boy, I was certainly taken by her. I offered to get her some water and perhaps some Advil, which she agreed she could use. Back across the street I went. She drank the water and took a pill, and when the blood had pretty much stopped, she was embarrassed about our collision.

I didn't want to just say goodbye and send her on her way, so instead I asked, "Hey, would you like to go back to my hotel with me? It's just up the street." I indicated the direction with a small wave of my hand.

She looked suddenly wary. "Um, I don't think that's such a good idea," she said with distant politeness.

"Oh! I didn't mean it like that," I spluttered, flustered in my realization that I hadn't meant to say what I had said. In a subconscious effort to cover my blunder, I started talking at twice my normal speed. "I didn't mean to imply, well, you know. It's just, there's a nice bar in the lobby. I don't know the area very well, so I thought it'd be easiest to go back there to get a cup of coffee or tea or something and just sit and relax or talk or—"

She laughed and gently cut me off. "That'd be nice."

I stared at her blankly for a moment, taken aback by her agreeing to hang out with me. Recovering, I smiled and led the way to the hotel, which was less than two blocks away.

Sammy was a very positive young lady. By the time we wandered into the lobby, she had shaken off the fall and her lip was nearly an undetectable injury. With her feeling better and both of us a little more relaxed, we started to get to know each other. She was 19 years old, going to college in Atlanta, and preferred to be called "Sammy" rather than her full name, "Samantha," because it "didn't sound nearly as stuffy." She had driven to Memphis for a few days to visit her cousin. Sammy had to leave the next morning, but since her cousin was working as a waitress that night, she was on her way to see a movie when we ran into each other. I was glad she was willing to choose me over the movie for the evening.

My previous plan was to get a good night's rest for tomorrow's tournament, but I found that I was in no rush to leave this beautiful young woman. We talked for hours, and I was more and more taken by her. I thought briefly of Max, who was committed to going to bed early this night, then swiftly pushed him from my mind.

"Now it's your turn," she stated matter-of-factly and squared herself to me. "So, I'll start with an obvious question: do you have a girlfriend?" She sipped her café latte and gave me the slightest quirk of her eyebrow.

I laughed. "Not at the moment."

"Have you had one before?" she asked teasingly.

"I've had a few girlfriends in the last couple of years. Most of the girls I get involved with are from school, and between golf and classes, my girlfriends never feel like I give them enough attention. After a few months, it's usually over."

"Hmm, so you're single and focused. Both good things to know." She grinned at me over her coffee cup.

"What about you?"

She smiled subtly. "I'm currently drifting between boys."

The conversation continued in this manner and we talked for hours. Although I felt like I'd known Sammy forever, I knew very little about her. I didn't know her last name, where she grew up, or anything about her family; but our conversation never became boring. She was young, sexy, smart, and sassy. She asked a lot of questions, but didn't offer much about herself.

Before we knew it, they were giving last call at the bar. She surprisingly looked at the clock on her phone. "Two in the morning! I really need to get back to my cousin's place. She lives outside the city, and it's going to be a drag getting out there."

I laid down some cash for the waiter and stood up. "That's fine. I need to try to get some sleep, anyway. I'll walk you to your car."

"You really don't have to do that."

"I insist. I can't let a girl wander around a strange city at two in the morning, especially after I've already done my best to beat her up."

Sammy giggled and rose to her feet. "Okay, fine! It's parked somewhere near where you tried to 'beat me up.'" She took the lead out of the hotel, and I was less than a step behind.

Back at the sight of our collision, she realized she didn't remember where her car was. She didn't know the area very well, and the city blocks all looked the same to her. We strolled for a while, and although we were on a mission to get her to her car, neither of us was terribly anxious to find it. We ended up at a park and decided we weren't going to get any sleep, anyway, so we made the most of the pleasant night. We found a bench and continued our conversation. We hadn't touched each other, but the stares between us were as romantic as any I had ever felt. I wanted to kiss her so badly my whole body seemed to ache, but I didn't want to scare her off. I had never been so taken by anyone.

We talked, walked some more, and the hours rolled past. We ended up back at my hotel at 6 am. She decided to take a cab home and would come back later in the day with her cousin to find her car. I had to get to the golf course, so I walked her to a cab out front. As we neared the car, I moved closer to her, put my hands on her shoulders, and planned to give her a small kiss goodbye. I was afraid to kiss her, but I knew I had to. I would sorely regret it if I didn't. Sammy didn't resist, and I moved my face closer to hers. She smelled wonderful. I pressed my lips to hers, and I left them there for a millisecond longer than I thought I should have, but she pleasantly pushed her lips harder against mine. We embraced and our mouths stayed together for a long time. I was ready to miss the day of golf and go wherever Sammy wanted. I would have done anything to stay with her, and I didn't want to leave. We melted into each other. She placed her head on my shoulder, and I felt her breasts and my rib cage come together. We kissed again, and I saw a tear run down her cheek. How could I let her go? We stayed there, making out in the street, for what seemed like hours. I felt the overwhelming urge to tell her that I loved her, which I had never said to any woman except my mother. I resisted the desire, but this beautiful young lady had given me feelings I didn't know existed, and I felt she was having a similar experience.

I pulled away and looked deep into her eyes. "I have to see you later," I said.

"Absolutely." She nodded and gave me a determined look. "I'll meet you this afternoon. I promise."

I grinned. "I'll be back here after the tournament, probably no later than 2:30."

She gave me a dazzling smile in return. "3 o'clock right here, then?"

"That'll be perfect, I'll have to meet the team bus here at five to make my flight, so that will give us a good couple of hours to hang out. Maybe we can grab a late lunch here at the hotel?"

"Call it breakfast because I'm going back to get some sleep." Sammy said with her smile moving into her voice.

"Oh, now I feel bad about keeping you up all night."

"Hey, I'm not the one having to go play golf. I should be apologizing to you for not letting you rest up for your big tournament."

"I'll be fine, it's only golf" I didn't want to let on how far from the truth that statement really is, but I would do anything to spend every last second I could with her.

"I doubt your coach would like to hear you say that."

"That's probably true." With golf suddenly brought back to mind, I instinctively looked at my watch. "Oh man, I probably need to get going."

She looked at me with those beautiful dark brown eyes, pulls my head towards hers, and we locked lips again for another minute-long kiss. I couldn't get enough of her. We finally pulled apart and stare into each other's eyes. I gave her my cell phone number, reluctantly pushing us toward our imminent separation. She promised to text me later and would meet me back at the hotel that afternoon.

Samantha kissed me one more time, smiled passionately, and jumped in the cab. I watched her pull away and thought to myself, *What the hell just happened?* I had never felt so alive. I sprinted to the room.

Max was astonished that I was just getting home. "We have to leave in fifteen minutes!"

"I swear I'll be ready!" I shouted in response, closing the door to the bathroom as I did so.

We got to the course, teed off after a quick warm up, and we were off. Max and I were paired with two players from Florida State. Max was anxious to hear all about my night, assuming I had been up all night with this girl having wild sex. So, when I said I had only kissed her goodbye, he didn't believe me. We played golf between me telling him every detail of the night, and I couldn't stop talking. I was exhausted, but I played like I was the best golfer in the world. It was like I couldn't do anything wrong. We didn't say one word to the guys from Florida, and it seemed like I was making every putt I hit. Max played well, and it wasn't until after the first nine holes that I realized he hadn't thrown a single club.

I looked at him and said, "You're playing pretty well today."

"Are you kidding?" he said to me, "I shot even par 36 on the front. Do you have any idea what you shot?"

I didn't have a clue. With Sammy in my head, there wasn't room for remembering things like how many times I'd hit a golf ball. All I could recall of the front nine was telling Max every little detail of this perfect young lady, and I'm sure he must have been bored to death not hearing about any crazy sexual encounters.

"Jim, you made nine straight birdies! Shot 27 on the front. You shattered the course record for the front nine!"

"Are you kidding?!" I was oblivious, exhausted, excited, and confused.

He laughed outright. "I really wish I was."

I was flabbergasted. I had made good runs in the past, putting together nine hole rounds of five or six under par, but I had never birdied every hole.

Jack was there at the turn. He was obviously aware of what I had done, but he knew better than to mess with a hot streak. Honestly, he should have said something reassuring. My head started spinning, and I convinced myself I needed to get my mind on the game by putting Sammy out of it until later. I had the round of my life going, and I needed to focus.

Well, focus I did. I thought through every shot, concentrated with every drop of energy I had. Max was afraid to say anything to me as my attitude changed. I played like a man possessed. I didn't even know there were three others playing with me. However, the more I "focused," the worse I played, and the more my lack of sleep started catching up to me. I finished the back nine with a five over par 41, still shot 68, and won the tournament; but I could have shot that infamous 54. I forgot everything I had learned and ruined the round of a lifetime. I hadn't shot 41 for nine holes in a long time.

What the hell went wrong? I really didn't need to ask that question. It was obvious. On the front nine, I wasn't thinking golf. I was on autopilot, just going through the motions, thinking of a girl, and playing my absolute best. I put my "head in the game" on the back nine and totally screwed it up.

It was an invaluable lesson; stick to the topic of girls and don't think about golf during a tournament. I went back to the hotel completely exhausted and depressed. I then realized Samantha was going to be there at 3:00, which would give me another two hours with her before I had to leave with the team to catch our plane. That thought gave me the energy to go take a shower and wait for her in the lobby. I arrived at the lobby bar at 2:58. I was very impressed I had gotten there as quickly as I did. I had completely forgotten she was going to send me a text message, and when I looked for my phone, I remembered it was turned off and still in my golf bag. My mind was a total blur as I ran to the room to get it. I was back in the bar by 3:02 and convinced myself she would be there no matter how late I was. I sat back at the bar and ordered a double espresso. I don't normally drink espressos, but I figured I could use the caffeine. I had turned my phone on in the elevator, and it was just now coming up. It showed I had two voicemails and three text messages. The first voicemail was from my father, wishing me well in today's tournament. The second was from a girl I took out last week at school, also wishing me well and hoping we could get together when I got home later that night. I knew I would never call her again after meeting Sammy. All three text messages were from a "private number," which turned out to be Sammy's.

The first had come in within minutes of her leaving this morning in the cab. She sent a picture of herself, and she looked tired but beautiful. She, too, wished me luck in the tournament. The second came at 1:03 pm and was taken in her cousin's car. It also came up as a private number, and it dawned on me that I didn't have any information on her. I didn't know her last name, couldn't retrieve her phone number, and only prayed she'd show up. But from the looks of her text messages, I figured she was the real deal. The text said they were going to get her car, she had to run an errand, and she would see me at 3:00. The third message was a picture taken inside her car. She was driving the green Nissan Maxima we had been looking for, and apparently, she found it just a few blocks from where we met. She was so sexy looking. She obviously had a chance to get a little rest and fix herself up since the morning, and she sent me a picture of herself with one hand on the wheel and a huge smile on her face. Her hair was covering a little of her face; and as I stared at her picture, the mess I made of the back nine became a thing of the past. This girl was so incredible, if only I had kept my mind on her through all eighteen holes, it could have been the perfect round of golf. Right then, though, it didn't seem to matter. I knew she would arrive any moment, and somehow we were going to figure out the world in the next two hours.

Underneath the picture in her third text was the caption, "Jim b thr soon! xo Sammy," and it had come in at 2:26 pm. The espresso was suddenly like a bolt of energy. I never drank much caffeine, and this reminded me why. It was like someone had injected me with an overdose of nervousness. I became jumpy and anxious for her to arrive. I paid the bartender and decided to walk around and wait for her, hoping maybe the movement would work off some of the caffeine. I paced around the lobby a few times and peered outside for the car I had spent hours looking for last night. Sammy was so thorough in describing it to me during our stroll through the city twelve hours ago that I could recite every fine detail from the scratch on the passenger side door handle to the funny little ding on her back-license plate.

Where was she? It was now 3:13. I had less than two hours to be on the van leaving for the airport, and with finals starting, I couldn't be late returning to Charlotte. I had previously tried to figure out how I could stay another day with Sammy and get back later on Monday, but it wasn't a smart plan. I figured there were only two more weeks of school, and then both she and I would have the summer free. We would be able to find a way to spend as much time together as possible over the summer. I knew she had turned my life upside-down in just one night, and nothing I had previously planned for the summer months was going to be the same.

Jack came walking through the hotel lobby and saw me pacing around. "Jim, why aren't you getting some rest? We have to leave in an hour, and you look like shit."

It was true. I hadn't slept all night, I had the worst and best emotional rollercoaster ride of my life in the last 19 hours, the double espresso was doing nothing but adding to my stress and nervous energy, and Sammy still hadn't pulled up in front of the hotel yet.

Jack wanted to talk about my round of golf today. He needed me to tell him what the heck happened out there, how the tale of two completely different rounds of golf had occurred on back-to-back nines. I kept looking around for Sammy as I gave him the Cliff Notes summary version of what went on, and Jack eventually asked if I was in some kind of trouble. I didn't have the time to explain everything to him. She was going to be here any minute, and the debriefing of today's round of golf would take hours of discussion between Jack and me. I told him I would tell him all about it on the plane. He shook his head and told me to at least make sure I was ready to go when it was time to catch the bus. He glanced at his watch. "Which means," he said, "that you only have about an hour and a half to get all your crap together."

An hour and a half? Only 90 minutes?! Where the hell was she! Sammy was now half an hour late. I tried to retrieve her number from my phone, but it simply wasn't possible. I called my cell phone company and asked them how to do it. I was practically frantic with the operator and insisted there was a way to get it. I nearly resorted to threatening the poor girl on the other end of the line if she didn't give me that number. She could tell how stressed I was getting, and was very nice about telling me that they didn't have access to blocked phone numbers any more than I did. I hung up on her and went back outside to look for Sammy. What could possibly have gone wrong? Did something happen to her on the way to the hotel? I thought about calling the State Patrol to see if there had been any accidents, but I didn't even know her last name. They surely wouldn't give me any information on a green sedan involving a girl named Samantha without more information. They would think I was crazy if I told them I was her boyfriend and didn't know her last name.

It was almost 4:00, and I was now both mad and confused. The espresso was practically making my eyes bug out of my head, and I felt like I was wearing a hole in the carpet along the stretch of floor I kept pacing over. Max came down looking for me because Jack had told him I looked strange and acted crazy when we talked. He saw me in the front of the hotel and knew I was in trouble.

Max approached me slowly and calmly said, "Hey, Jim, you really need to relax. Why don't you come upstairs and start getting ready to leave?" He knew I was crazy about this girl I barely knew, and I could tell by his countenance that my mania was painful for him to watch.

"I can't, Max," I responded, trying my best not to sound too pathetic. "Please, can you pack up my golf bag for me?"

He hesitated a moment, then nodded, obviously resigned to the fact that this was probably the only way he was going to be able to help. "Yeah, I can do that. What about the rest of your stuff?"

"Thanks, you're the absolute best. You can just throw everything else into my travel bag. It doesn't have to be neat, just get it all in there." Max was truly more than a friend. The four years we'd spent together had been like becoming brothers, and when a family member is in trouble, you do what you have to do.

The next hour passed with no sign of Sammy, and despite my better judgment, I called the two local hospitals with no luck whatsoever and thought better of calling the police. I was given the run-around, just like I'd expected, without being able to give them her last name. I was yelling at the phone, saying they needed to help me, but I knew I sounded deranged. As nicely as they could, they basically hung up on me. Jack and Max were now in the lobby with the rest of the golf team, the van was pulling up front, and we had to leave. Everyone was tip-toeing around me, not sure what was wrong, but after shooting 27 / 41, they were all afraid I'd snapped. It was like they were trying to get a mental patient on the bus to the crazy ward.

We left for the airport on the van. There was still no sign of Sammy, and my mind was going crazy. I was saying things to myself, and half of it was coming out of my mouth. Nobody knew what I was talking about except Max. He saw my pain, and he did his best to keep everyone away from me while simultaneously telling me to relax, try to rest. "She'll call soon," he muttered comfortingly, "and you'll figure it out with her. She must have had car trouble," he continued, "and her cell phone probably ran out of battery since she hadn't charged it last night…" He stayed in this vein for quite some time, and he had a way of making me believe him. We would fly home, and before I knew it, Sammy and I would spend hours and hours on the phone reliving last night and getting to know each other better. We would have the entire summer to be together. Max was so reassuring that I finally calmed down. The trip seemed like it took much less time than it actually did. I must have slept in between moments of consciousness. Thankfully, Jack realized the plane ride wasn't the time for our discussion, and he kept his distance. We landed, and Max somehow got me back to our dorm room, where I promptly passed out on my bed.

\*\*\*

I gradually shift my attention back from the past to the present. I use my radar gun to measure the yardage to the pin, and it reads 157 yards. I move in over my ball, preparing to hit the tee shot to this shorter par 3, and out of the corner of my eye I spot the metal yardage marker with a bold "154" emblazoned on its face. As hard as I'm trying not to think of shooting the infamous 54, that number is haunting me!

I step away from my ball and regroup my thoughts. The shot at hand is downhill over water to a middle pin. I do my best to focus solely on the pin, knowing that if shooting 54 becomes the focus, the reality of doing so will disappear faster than the thought can manifest in my imagination. I hit a hard eight iron, hoping to put it past the pin and spin it back toward the water. It's a risky shot, but I'm feeling confident and pull it off to perfection. Both Max and Dustin hit on the green long. They don't get the spin I achieve and leave themselves with much longer birdie putts than my 13 feet. As we walk off down the hill, I ask Max what happened next with Vanessa. I don't want to let on that somehow I know they are still together, and I have a feeling that I am going to meet this lovely little redhead in the near future. Max has never talked about any woman like this, and as much as he tries to play it off as one of his many conquests, he isn't fooling me. He downplays any "relationship" he may have with Vanessa, but goes on to tell me how they see each other from time to time.

Dustin is first to putt, and I have to move my ball marker one putter-head length to the left to get it out of his line. I know I will get a good read off his putt. I stand off at a 90-degree angle so I don't disturb him and watch as closely as I can to see where his ball passes my ball mark and where—in relation to the hole—it finishes. A long putt like Dustin's is very beneficial to me if the shot doesn't drop, since it makes it easier to determine how far it breaks off-line. Dustin's ball passes about 6 inches right of my ball mark and comes to rest less than a cup-width left of the hole. He hit the perfect putt to give me a read without standing in his line. I move my mark back as Max prepares to hit his slightly shorter putt from the opposite side of the green, and I don't even need to watch his putt to know what mine is going to do. Max gets it close, maybe 15 inches short, and right of the cup. Both he and Dustin make an easy par three, and I have, once again, another makeable birdie putt. It is a slightly downhill, right-to-left breaker of maybe five inches, roughly 13 feet to negotiate a four-under-through-four-hole start. I have done it before, and I know it is going in. I purposefully put the image of Vanessa standing there naked by the pool with all those people watching in my head, and I can see everything as Max described it. I know this is a more useful image than over thinking this easy little putt. See the girl, see the line, make the stroke, and bang! There it is in the bottom of the cup. Four under!

Max knows me so well, he looks at me and asks simply, "You could see her naked, couldn't you?"

"Yep," I say, "right to the bottom of the cup."

Hole #5

Par 4 – 456 yards

"So, does she look as good in real life as she does in my imagination?" I ask Max.

"Jim, you're going to have to meet this one."

I seriously can't remember ever meeting one of Max's girls after he was done with her. Don't get me wrong, Max is a great guy and I've always thought someday he would stop running around and settle down, but I am not quite ready to fully grasp the idea the time has come. We have had so much fun chasing women over the years, and it has made for great conversations all through our careers.

I have the honor of teeing off first. The image of Vanessa is still in my mind, and I hit the driver with a tempo I was used to in my prime. I smooth it up the right-center of the fairway, close to 300 yards. Max pulls his drive into the left-hand rough. He'll have a difficult time hitting the green from there. Large oak trees line the left side of the fairway, and he'll have to negotiate hitting under a low ceiling of orange and red leaves overhanging that area. Dustin pipes one down the center of the fairway almost 20 yards past mine. During our conversations, Max and I have been so engrossed that I haven't noticed Dustin getting mad. He's not beating me, and the sheer fury in his tee shot is a loud reminder to me that he intends to win this event.

"Well, now that you've seen my lady naked in your head, why don't you tell me about this little hussy you've been hanging out with?" Max says to me.

"This one could take a little longer than the 13 holes we have left," I told him. "Let's get started."

***

After college, Max went out on some of the mini tours. He struggled to make a few cuts and spent all his money chasing different events, and different women, around the country for a couple of years. His father helped him as much as he could, but without securing sponsors with deep pockets, Max wasn't able to bring his career to the PGA tour like he'd hoped. Being a top collegiate golfer wasn't nearly as hard as making it out on the tour, and Max had the game but couldn't keep it together mentally for the full four days of each event. He made a few good runs, but it wasn't enough. I actually think he didn't want it as much as he thought he did. Once he settled into his job, golf became more fun for him without all the expectations hanging over his head. He was making a good living and living a great life. Whenever I was particularly stressed the past few years, I sometimes caught myself wishing that I had gone into the golf business like he did.

Instead, as soon as I graduated from college, I went to Atlanta and back to Memphis to try to find Samantha. I followed every lead I could, and ended up with nothing. It was like she never existed. Max knew what I was doing, but I told my parents I wanted to take a little post-graduation road trip through the South and take some time to enjoy not having to be anywhere. I went to every restaurant in Memphis asking every waitress if they had a cousin named Sammy. I tried to search college records at the schools in Atlanta, but never got anywhere. I finally gave up, went back home to my folks' place, and followed through with my plan to go to medical school. I knew golf wasn't going to be a career for me. I think I could have been like Max and run around chasing the dream, but I got a lot of golf out of my system in college. I always believed golf was the game of a lifetime and wanted to enjoy it for as long as I could. I didn't need to prove anything. I had accomplished more than I ever expected, and it brought me pleasures I would have forever.

So, I started med school in the fall at the University of Miami. I figured I could at least play golf all winter instead of going to school in Boston, where I was also accepted. My parents helped with expenses, since I managed to get undergraduate taken care of with my golf scholarship. Medical school was a lot of work, and I was fortunate to not have to have a job to get through it. I didn't play nearly as much golf as I planned, but I did manage to hustle a game or two every now and then in Miami to put some extra cash in my pocket. I never forgot about Sammy. I played that night over and over in my head for years, and she actually got me through med school when times were tough. As I spent countless all-nighters studying, I reminded myself of shooting the best nine holes of my life without any sleep at all.

I spent all four years in Miami working my tail off. I was committed to learning all that I could about the medical industry. It was the hardest time of my life, and I wished I had studied more in undergrad. Not that I would have given up any of the golf, but there was no doubt that it didn't prepare me for medical school. I dated girls off and on, but didn't have the time like I did in North Carolina. Every once in a while, Max would pass through town and we would squeeze in a round or two on the course, but my game had taken a backseat and his was in top shape.

***

Max's ball is sitting in the thick rough. It is all he can do to advance it 100 yards down the fairway, and he leaves himself a good chance to get up and down, but it will take some skill. I have 170 yards to a back pin on a long and narrow green. I hit a hard seven iron and overcook it just a bit. It heads left toward a greenside bunker, but as today's luck would have it, it bounces off the right side of the bunker right toward the pin and rolls up to less than a foot from the hole.

Max grins at me and motions with his head toward Dustin, who is not at all happy for me. The steam coming out of his ears is almost visible as he tries to prepare to hit his next shot. I feel bad for him. The kid has the game, but he hasn't learned how to manage his emotions. As if to illustrate this revelation, he snap-hooks his nine iron left of the bunker into the deep rough. It is a terrible mistake, and bogey will be a great score from there if he can calm himself down. I can't help but think that maybe if he joined in on our conversation, he might be the one four under par at this point, instead of me. However, it's obvious he won't want to hear that right now.

We begin walking down the fairway to the green, and I start telling Max about Cindy, who happens to be the "little hussy" he was unwittingly referring to.

***

Cynthia Smith was from Malibu, California. She was moving to Boston, and her mother was driving cross-country with her to help her get settled. She was an only child, adopted by an older couple at birth, didn't have much idea about her paternal mother or father, and only when she was in college did she even look into it. She found out a little about her real mother, but didn't go any further. She felt lucky this couple had found her because she grew up in a wonderful home with two loving parents. Her father had just turned fifty when she was adopted, and he died when she was a freshman in college. He had a bad heart most his adult life but didn't let it slow him down. He raised Cindy to be a great athlete, teaching her to play all kinds of sports. They would water ski, snow ski, hike, bike, play baseball, football, soccer, and even some golf. You name it, she played it. He was there for her right up until he had a massive heart attack and died at 69 years old. Her mother was a few years younger and never worked a day in her life. They married when she graduated college, and for over 25 years, they traveled while he worked as a consultant to overseas companies in the oil and gas business. They were nearly retired when they adopted Cindy, and they had the means to live a life anyone would be envious of without being over-the-top about it.

When Cindy was moving to Boston, she was 29 years old, working as a graphic artist, and had just been offered a job in a top firm in Boston. Her mother didn't want her moving so far away, but she knew it was a great opportunity, so they packed up her car and headed east. Her mom was going to stay a month or so, and then figured she would eventually move there once Cindy settled into her job. They were very close, and despite a large age difference, they truly were best friends.

***

Max has a 60 yard shot straight to the flag. He hits a low spinner right on-line, but the ball hits once, jumps toward the pin, and spins back down over a ridge in the green to about 50 feet away. He shows a little frustration, but all in all, I am amazed how well he is handling his bad shots. This is something he never did in the past.

Dustin's ball is sitting in as bad a lie as you could wish on your worst enemy, and I feel for him. He wants to win this so badly, but he can't buy a break. He takes a huge swing, trying to hit a flop-shot over the bunker to a tight pin. He lurches at his ball and slides his club under it, expecting the ball to pop straight up onto the green, but the ball never moves. The rough is so deep and thick that his club goes directly under the ball and misses it completely. It's almost sad to watch his anger destroy any potential he had. He immediately swings again and lands the ball directly in the bunker. He slams his club to the ground and yells, "FUCK!" I can see his parents far off the side of the green, trying to hide their embarrassment. There must be a lot of family pressure, and this game isn't going to have a good outcome for him unless something changes drastically in the next few holes.  He hits a great sand shot to three feet and makes a double-bogey six.

Max leaves his putt a good eight feet short, but is able to salvage bogey by making the next one.  My one-foot tap-in birdie is too easy, and I am enjoying this round of golf as much as any I have ever played.

Hole #6

Par 4 – 377 yards

This hole has a hard dog-leg to the right and is slightly uphill, but you can shave off the corner by flying over the huge, magnificently fall-colored trees on the right side of the fairway. I hit a towering three wood with a slight fade up over the corner, and my ball rolls through the far side of the fairway into the first cut of rough. This is the first fairway I've missed today, but I have a good lie and a great angle to the pin. Max has always been able to move the ball left-to-right as well as anyone I've ever played with. He pulls his driver, bombs it around the corner with a solid slice, and puts it within 40 yards of the green. Dustin wants to hit a similar shot, but cuts off too much of the corner. His ball hits a tree and comes to rest deep in the forest.

\*\*\*

I had been working as an anesthesiologist for the past three years at Massachusetts General in downtown Boston. I did a one-year internship at Jackson Memorial in Miami prior to being accepted into this program where I did my four-year residency before being hired on as a full-time attending physician. In addition to my practice in the hospital, I still work a lot in the emergency room. There's an excitement in the ER which has always kept my interest and given me the satisfaction of giving back to my community in my own way. I rented a great townhome twenty minutes north of the hospital, and there are a handful of great golf courses nearby. I didn't have many expenses, and I was suddenly making a good living and greatly enjoying my job at the hospital. I could play golf at least two or three days a week, there were plenty of young nurses to keep me entertained, and I was content in every way possible.

It was a long day in late July when Cindy was admitted to the hospital.

43

I had been helping with a handful of different surgeries in the O.R. that day, and I was looking forward to getting off work and having a beer. The chief of surgery paged me and asked that I please stay on for this one last case. He knew I had already worked a long day, but he was short-staffed and promised he'd make it up to me. We have always gotten along well, and he insisted he wanted me and not one of the residents handling this case, because it sounded like it was going to be complicated.

When I got to the O.R., all I could see of Cindy were her eyes. She and her mother had been in a terrible car crash, and she was unconscious with severe head trauma. Her long brown hair had been cut away on the right side of her head to reveal a massive wound that was bleeding out of control. I had to work around the surgeons to get her properly sedated so they could tend to the injury. We were in surgery for seven hours while we put her back together. She had also suffered two broken ribs, a fractured left leg, and a severely broken pinky on her right hand. In summary, she was a mess. The accident had totaled her car and the other car, as well. The only person from the other car was in the room next door, also with a head injury; but I later found out it wasn't nearly as bad. At the end of the seven hours, we had to induce a coma to keep her alive. With the amount of swelling in her brain we knew she'd be comatose for at least a week or two, and with her injuries, that would be better for her, anyway. She would still be in a lot of pain whenever she woke up, but the worst part will be giving her the bad news. Her mother hadn't survived the crash. She was pronounced dead at the scene.

\*\*\*

Max is in shock at the direction of this story. He can't believe this comatose girl is who I want to talk about during the tournament. But for me, there is no one else I want to think of until the last putt drops on the eighteenth green. And there's still a mountain of recollections to get through before we get there.

***

During the time Cindy was in surgery, I kept looking at her eyes. They seemed vaguely familiar, but I couldn't place where I might have met her. She sort of reminded me of a girl who worked in the hospital, but her injuries made her features fairly unrecognizable. While she was being worked on, everyone was too busy for me to truly scrutinize her face; and afterward, she was so bandaged I could only see her eyes. But there was something in those eyes that kept tugging at the corners of my mind, despite being closed.

I would visit her daily in the intensive care unit. She was going to be in a coma for a few weeks, and I kept thinking about how this poor woman was going to wake up to find out her mother died in the car crash she herself had barely survived. She would have months of recovery with her broken bones, and there was much uncertainty about how alert she will be when she comes out of the coma. The hospital social workers along with the Boston police were searching for any additional family members for Cynthia Smith. However, her mother was listed as her only family in every record they dug up. I spent many hours thinking about her, and I couldn't imagine all the pieces of her life she would need to put back together when she recovered.

It was unusual for an anesthesiologist to spend so much time following up on a case like this, and the ICU nurses took notice. They often commented as I walked into the ward, but they never stopped me. Perhaps they thought it was a blessing she had at least one consistent visitor. Cindy was now the responsibility of the hospital staff, and although she was in good hands, she didn't have an assigned doctor. Whichever resident was on duty would oversee her during that shift, and the same was true of the nurses. The staff social workers were busy trying to find insurance money for her, and they eventually abandoned the futile search for additional family. If the police hadn't found her driver's license in the car, she would have been just one of the many Jane Does we have come through every year.

As the weeks went on, I continued to visit her. I wouldn't really do anything except stop in her room, look at her for a moment, and move on. At first, I looked at her chart and spoke with the doctor on duty, but there wasn't much to be told; still comatose, injuries were healing, the brain damage was uncertain, but there were expectations she could fully recover. The induced coma was only temporary, but we knew it was entirely up to her body as when she would come out of it. We couldn't do anything to speed the process along. I learned many years ago that as a doctor, you can't get emotionally involved with a patient. You have to look at it like a mechanic working on a car; you do what you can to fix the vehicle at hand and then move on to all the other cars in need of your attention. Getting attached to those who are dying or grievously injured only takes away from your ability to help others. With this knowledge as my only defense, I was actively resisting my emotional desire to learn more about Cindy. However, there was something intriguing about her that slowly kept eating away at my resolve.

***

We help Dustin find his ball, shuffling through the rough and trees trying to locate the little white orb. It has settled at the base of a large oak tree, leaving his only option a chip backward to the fairway. If he hits it far enough back, he can leave an opportunity to get around the corner and reach the green. He does a decent job, but I feel like he should have studied the shot a few moments longer, gotten his frustration out of his head, and minimized his losses. But I know that the proper play is always easier to see when it's not yours.

Dustin rushes the shot out of anger, and he'll be feeling it on the next shot. He picks up his clubs and stalks backward out of the woods to his ball. Max and I go in the other direction toward our own golf balls.

"So, why so much interest in this girl, Jim?" he asks as we step over tree stumps toward the fairway.

It's a fair question. Max practically went through medical school with me. We talked all the time, and he was a reliable support when I needed to vent my frustrations. He heard all the disgusting stories, and he somehow seemed to love them. But as he knows well, he doesn't have the stomach to go through it himself. I've told him so many stories of cases in the past, but I never mentioned any names. It was always, "This guy with a gunshot wound to the head..." or, "Some lady who lost an arm..." This story was different, and Max is unsure of what direction it was heading.

"I told you it was going to take some time to get through this story," I reprimand lightly. "You're just going to have to hear me out."

We watch Dustin hit his third shot, and he is able to get it close to the front of the green where he will have a chance to make a long putt for par. I get to my ball, and it is sitting up in a fluffy lie on the first cut of rough. I only have 74 yards straight to the pin, and I have enough confidence in my swing that I focus solely on the hole. I hit a smooth sand wedge with a slightly choked-down grip and throw the ball right at the pin. I know it won't spin from this lie, and I aim ten yards short of the flag. It lands as planned and releases toward the hole. I couldn't have hit it any better. It rolls up to five feet from the target. I am really on today! I watch the ball come to a stop and look at Max, who is grinning at me. He holds my gaze for a longer-than-normal time to let me know that I'm on fire. I smile back and motion to him to hit his ball. He waves me off, takes a good look at his easy chip to the green, and snuggles his shot close to the pin, as I knew he would.

"Tell me she recovered and now you're sleeping with her," Max says to me.

"Not that easy," I reply as we walk to the green to get out of Dustin's way. "Don't rush me. I want you to hear the whole story." We put our clubs down just off the green, and Dustin hits a good putt, but nobody expects him to make it. He leaves himself about 8 feet on my same line, for which I'm always appreciative. I glance at Dustin to see if he will accept my gratitude, but he never looks up. He slams the ball into the hole. Good thing he made it, otherwise he would still be away. His putt was straight in, and I follow the same line. Sure enough, I make it without any problem. Max has just a few feet and negotiates for another birdie.

We have a long walk over to the seventh tee box, and I use the time to continue telling my story to Max.

***

On day 22 after Cindy was first admitted to the hospital, I entered her room and could see her face for the first time. They had finally removed the large bandages for good. The nurses had taken them off before, but then reapplied new ones when I wasn't around, so I never saw her. I came up short at the sight of her. This couldn't be the same girl I'd been visiting for over three weeks. I blinked rapidly a few times, looked to see if her face had changed in the last three seconds, decided it hadn't, and reached for her chart. It still said "Cynthia Smith." The room started to spin, and I had to sit quickly in the visitor's chair as I felt all the blood rush out of my head. The face framed by the sterile hospital pillows was Sammy's. Sexy, mysterious, gone-from-my-life-forever Samantha.

I took a few deep breaths and tried to collect my thoughts. It was eerie that a girl I barely knew and only spent half a day with, who had haunted my thoughts for the last ten years, was now laying here in front of me. No, it was beyond eerie. It was *impossible*. Yet here she apparently was. Could Cynthia really be Samantha? Or was it just my imagination and years of longing skewing my senses? Everything started spinning again. In the weeks that had passed, I never once thought she might be Sammy. There was something in her eyes that drew me toward her, but the thought of Sammy never once occurred to me. Could she have lied to me about her name a decade ago? Or perhaps she didn't like Cynthia and decided to go by Samantha? Was it truly possible for this to be the same girl? I didn't know what to do. I felt sick. The ICU nurse who had been overly friendly came into the room and asked if I was alright. I must have looked like I had seen a ghost.

I said, "I think I know her".

She responded, "We all figured you did, since you come by so often." This was fair. There had been all kinds of speculation about me and the "coma girl," stemming from my numerous visits to her bedside, but I had dismissed it as idle gossip. Maybe they were right.

"I hadn't really been able to see her face before now," I told her. "Do we know anything more about her?"

There hadn't been any new information. They had her name, social security, an address in California, and an insurance company that was paying her claims. That was it. I was slowly regaining control over myself. I looked back down at her chart, but this time to see any new information about her condition listed there. There was some updated brain wave activity showing she could come out of the coma at any time, but there was still too much uncertainty to accurately predict when that would be.

I asked the nurse to make me a copy of her information, which she did. As one of the doctors working on her case, there wouldn't be any reason to refuse. I decided right then that I was going to get the staff security people to run some additional information for me. It was not an unusual request, with all the unidentified patients we get, and the security staff has access to police records and full cooperation from law enforcement to help with such requests.

I stood close to her bedside and peered closely at her. With all the clinical disconnect I had cultured through my years of working as a doctor, I moved the blanket to better see her full torso. She was still covered in her gown, and I only wanted to see her frame. It had been ten years, but I remembered how Sammy was built. I thought if I could see her, then maybe it would help my recollection of her. As much as half of me was praying for this to be the same girl, the other half wasn't so sure I wanted her to be. I had spent years wondering if I'd ever see Sammy again, but this was never how it played out in my mind. Her body looked like what I remembered. That face was absolutely the same. Hair color, nose, everything told me this was Sammy.

The nurse helped me cover her back up. "Is it her?" she asked.

"I don't know. It sure looks like her, but I haven't seen her in a decade." I pause for a moment, hesitating. "And she doesn't have the same name."

I made sure they had my cell phone number listed on her chart with instructions to contact me as soon as she woke up. I thanked the nurse, and then went back to work. I had to get to the O.R. for another case. I thought about going to the chief and asking for the rest of the day off, but decided it would be better to finish my shift and see the security staff afterward.

***

# Hole #7

## Par 3 – 210 yards

We get to the tee and Max is stunned. "Is it her? Is it *her*?!" he keeps asking.

I refuse to answer. He is going to have to hear the whole story.

This hole is a long par three over water. A little wind is in our faces, and the pin is all the way back. I decide to hit a three hybrid and cut it into the wind, trying to get it to hit and stop. I look at Dustin, who is definitely the third wheel, and can see he is getting curious about our conversation. I sense he knows that if he can get his mind on whatever it is we're talking about, his game will get better. However, I'm not ready to share Cindy with a complete stranger yet.

I pull off the shot just as I see it and leave myself close to a 15-foot putt straight at the pin. Max still looks confused, and I'm not sure if it's my shot or my story that's the problem. He tries to gather his head while teeing up his ball. He looks at me, and I can see all he wants to do is hit his shot and start asking questions. He hits a four iron with absolute authority. His ball hits the middle of the green, but it doesn't make it over a ridge and it comes backwards to the front of the green. He should still be able to make an easy par from there, with as well as he putts. He doesn't even watch his ball stop, but instead walks next to me to not disturb Dustin and gives me the "what happened next" look; but I hold my finger to my lips and motion to Dustin. Max doesn't remove his eyes from me while Dustin hits a smooth hybrid to the back of the green and has one of his better opportunities for a birdie yet.

"Okay," I say, "so I went to the head of hospital security and started telling him my story."

\*\*\*

David Johnson was the man in charge, and I previously had had very few dealings with him in the past. But he's a golfer, and I promised a round of eighteen holes to get him to look into this for me. It wasn't out-of-line to do this kind of research on a patient, but I knew I was being an inconvenience by asking him to do it so quickly. He did some preliminary research and decided that he would, in fact, be able to find out more. He had done a little time in Washington DC working for a security company out of college, so he had experience getting around the government agencies, which would help him immensely now.

***

"There's no way this can be the same girl," Max says to me. "Don't tell me the girl of your sleepless nights is still in a coma and you know nothing more about her."

"It gets complicated," I tell him.

***

David was able to track Cynthia Smith to her hometown in California where she was adopted by her late parents. She was their only child, and there was no other family on record. Apparently, her parents hadn't maintained a relationship with any of their relatives, so there were no living grandparents and no additional family members. The adoption records were going to be more difficult to work with. There were international circumstances and a lot of information to sort through, since it initially looked like Cindy was brought to America from somewhere in Europe. This wasn't uncommon in the early 1980's, because birth parents had begun to reverse their decisions to give their children up. Numerous courts in the US sided against the adoptive families, which made many American couples start searching the globe for other options rather than risk having their would-be children reclaimed by the biological families.

***

On the green, Max has a very long uphill putt to a back pin. The turf breaks both directions, but I fully expect him to snuggle it up close and tap in for par. He is away and prepares for his shot. He seems out of his routine and doesn't take as much time as he should. I want to say something to draw his focus back, but it's against the rules and I don't want to cause either of us a penalty. When we talk on the golf course, we always make sure—if there was another player or someone else around us—that we speak loudly enough so they knew we are discussing something other than golf and that there isn't any sort of coaching going on between us. But at the same time, we never let any others hear enough of our conversation to let them in on our discussion. It is an art we perfected long ago.

Max makes a fast stroke of his putter and never gets the ball started on the right line. It catches a ridge he needs to be left of, and instead, the ball starts moving to the right almost immediately, away from his intended line. Max looks like he is going to snap his putter in two, but at the point where he absolutely needs to take a breath, he does. Then, even more surprisingly, he somehow manages to calm himself down without any real consequences. However, he still has 20 feet left to the hole and is still the farthest away. He gathers his head, studies the putt, walks around it from every angle, and focuses on making it this time. He hits a much better putt, but it doesn't drop. Rather, it slips by on the high side and misses by only the slightest of margins. He taps in and makes bogey. I refuse to look at him; I don't want to give him any reason to let more emotion into his head. Even though I am competing against him, I have such a huge lead already that I'm not actively trying to beat him.

Dustin, on the other hand, is doing a perfectly good enough job of beating himself. He has a real makeable birdie putt, just outside of mine from the other side of the green. He gets it started on-line, but it runs out of gas just a few inches short of dropping in the cup. I remind myself not to make that same mistake. My putt is uphill, and I can be aggressive with it. Dustin taps in for par, and I have this perfect vision of Samantha come into my head. I can see her like it was the morning I left her for the golf course ten years ago. Despite the years I spent wondering about her, there is always this calming effect I get when I think of her. I kneel down behind my ball, study the line, and can see it as perfectly as though there is a trench dug into the green between my ball and the cup. I just know I'll make it. Putting it seems like a mere formality; and sure enough, the next time I look up, it is dropping into the cup.

Hole # 8

Par 5 – 598 yards

The eighth hole isn't really reachable in two. There is a stream crossing the fairway twenty yards short of the green, and it is too much to negotiate. Even the longest players generally lay up to a good distance for their third shot, which is usually a full wedge. I hit an easy driver down the middle, making sure to hit the fairway. Distance isn't terribly important, since I plan to play it as a three-shot hole, anyway. Dustin is up next and hits a full driver as hard as he can. I realized he fully plans on going for the green in two, and I am curious to see what he will do. His ball is a good forty yards past mine, and I get the impression he's taking a lot of pride in that.

Max turns to Dustin and says, "Great shot." Knowing Max as well as I do, I immediately see the sarcasm wrapped around that statement, but it was well-hidden behind the charm he displays on the tee, and Dustin takes it as a sincere compliment. Max then steps up and hits a perfect three wood down the middle, just short of my ball. All three are in the fairway and in good shape.

As we walk off toward the fairway, Max winks at me and we share a conspiratorial smile. Dustin takes off ahead of us. His body language makes it apparent that his confidence has spiked since just missing birdie and bombing his driver past ours. Max slows his walking pace down a bit so we can talk some more.

***

David had found out a little about Cindy, and ended up having to request documents from the adoption agency in Pairs where he had tracked the records to. There was a hint of something in there from the Canadian government, but too much uncertainty at the time of the request. All signs

55

indicated it would take some time to get to the bottom of this mystery. Yet he seemed determined to find out as much as he could, which I was grateful for. Even if she came out of the coma today, there would be many weeks of hospital time left, which would hopefully give me enough time to figure out this mess. I wanted to be able to understand her a bit better, even if I didn't have any good news to give her.

I couldn't help but think that I didn't want to be there when Cindy woke up and have to be the one to tell her that her mother was dead. That thought kept me up many nights, but I wasn't sleeping much, regardless. My head wouldn't stop thinking just because I laid down with the intention of sleeping, and between working a more-than-full-time schedule at the hospital and doing my own research, I couldn't find enough hours in the day. I used to spend a lot of my time off playing golf, or at least trying to hit balls as often as possible. After a hard day of staring at bloody people in the operating room, hitting golf balls was the perfect relaxer I always yearned for. But with this project, I had neither the time nor the energy to get out to the course.

However, I did become an expert on adoption law over the next few days. A teammate of ours in college went to law school in Ohio and was practicing in New York. I stayed in touch with him via Facebook, and on the rare occasion we were in the same city, we would get in a round of golf. It had been two years since I last saw Rob but he was more than willing to help when I explained the situation. He was doing family law, so he was very familiar with adoptions. He gave me a few good websites to start with and offered to help further, which I politely accepted even though I felt I was already on the right track.

***

"What did Rob have to say?" Max asks. They were friendly to each other, but Max has never cared too much for Rob. Max thinks he isn't trustworthy, so he being an attorney seems to give Max some vindictive pleasure. It's like Max is happy that now everyone will see Rob the same way he does. Even still, I think Max is glad to know Rob was helping me out, since he does have a very well-respected law practice. Max has more distrust for Rob on the golf course than in the real world. There is something about a lost ball many years ago in a practice match with money on the line. I never actually heard the whole story, but I know if I were to bring it up now, Max could relive it as though it had happened this morning. Instead of having him relate his and Rob's ancient history to me, I change the subject and tell him about some of the difficulties involved with the international aspect of her adoption.

\*\*\*

With Rob's and David's help, I was able to track Cindy's birth parents to Montreal, Canada. Her birth mother was a young woman, only seventeen-years-old when she got pregnant. Her name was Crystal Wadel and she had been a bit promiscuous and had been with different men around the time she got pregnant. None of them were around by the time she figured it out, and she never planned on being a mother. She was five months pregnant before she recognized the symptoms, and she didn't know what to do about it. Eventually she decided she wanted to keep the baby, but when she went to her parents, they weren't at all supportive. She was alienated and told to leave. She was a disgrace to their family, and they wanted nothing more to do with her. She planned to move away, have her child and never see her family again.

\*\*\*

Walking down the fairway, I remind myself why I love this game so much; I'm spending the day with my best friend, playing a game we both love, the weather is perfect, and there is some of the most intense red and orange foliage imaginable framing the course. There is a moment where time seems to stand still, and it is like I am appreciating a piece of art. After all, this is nature's painting and I have been given the privilege of walking through it. Max is quiet for a moment, and I wonder what is going on in his head. I figure it to be something between finding a way to play better and finding a way to finally get me to the end of this story.

"She died," I told him frankly.

He turns pale as the words roll off my tongue. "Who died?!"

I stare at him, momentarily confused. "Oh! Sorry, Not Cindy! Her birth mother died during delivery, and Cindy was put up for adoption. That's all we were able to find out initially. It turns out there was some publicity about it in Montreal, so the adoption agency decided to send the baby to a European agency, thinking it would be better."

Max takes his stance over his ball and I shut my mouth. He is still in contention in this tournament, and as much as he wants to know more, I don't want to leave anything out. He hits a smooth five iron up the fairway, leaving his ball in the short grass with only a pitching wedge left to the green. It is the way to play the hole; three wood, five iron, wedge, and make the putt. I approach my ball. It is slightly ahead of Max's, and I feel I want to get just a bit closer to the green than Max did. My hope is to have a lob wedge of about eighty yards to the pin, which is on the front of the green. Another reason going for it in two isn't a smart choice is that even if you can get it over the creek, it's almost impossible to hold this green with a long iron or fairway wood. From the tee shot I hit, there isn't a decision to go for it, which is exactly why I hit it like I did. I take out my 21-degree hybrid and make a good, solid swing. It jumps off my club, and for a slight moment, I think I might have hit it too far. But it comes to rest inside the hundred-yard marker, which will be just right with that pin. Once I get up there, I only have 72 yards left. That leaves me with a smooth 64-degree lob wedge that I can put some spin on.

Dustin's parents have allowed themselves to remain a little closer to their son with his more positive attitude, and he is suddenly happier they are watching. His drive went well over 300 yards, and now it looks like he has about 280 yards from the pin. From what I can tell, he has a good 265 yards to carry over the creek, and he is undoubtedly going for it. I am anxious to see if he makes it over the water. It's possible, but I've seen more big numbers put up by getting cocky than by playing it a little more cautiously. I've never been one who wants to layup, but I've learned the hard way too many times on this particular hole that the layup is the way to play it. Dustin pulls a fairway wood, which looks like a three wood, and his parents look excited to see him play aggressively. I can only imagine growing up in his house, talking about "laying-up" at the dinner table and there being far too much testosterone in the house to even entertain the thought. Dustin jumps at it with too much power and never gets the club fully square to the ball, which starts heading to the right and keeps going. To give him credit, the ball probably could have made it if he hit it dead solid perfect; but as it is, his ball carries deep into the trees without much hope of ever seeing its player again. His parents are off that side of the fairway, and they immediately head in the direction of the ball with the hope they can help find it. They walk quickly in the line-of-flight, but I know it is going to be a futile search. You can see the steam rise from Dustin's head and I think he's going to explode. He reaches into his bag, grabs another ball, holds it out to his side, and drops it.

He says to Max and me, "I'm hitting a provisional for a lost ball. That was a number two, and this is a three." We nod our acknowledgement, and I think for sure he will reach down and grab a shorter iron to layup now, but no. He addresses the ball with both his three wood and all the anger in his body as he hits it again. This time, it goes straight at the pin and is a beautiful shot to watch. Unfortunately for Dustin, it doesn't make it across the creek. This is going to be a long hole.

Max and I really don't want to go look for his lost ball, but it is the right thing to do. We arrive where his parents are searching and start a halfhearted look through the thick woods. Dustin has five minutes from the time he arrives at the location to find his ball. There aren't any rules officials nearby, none of us players are wearing a watch, and neither of us are going to dig in our golf bags for a cell phone to time him so it's more a realistic amount of time we'll expect to look before Dustin calls it "lost". The pace of play is fine, we haven't had to wait on anyone all day, and nobody is closing in on us, so we have time to search. Dustin hasn't calmed down at all by the time he reaches us, and he no longer seems happy to have his family there to watch him fall apart. Personally, though, I think the more searchers we have for this wayward shot, the better.

I think Dustin and I could have become friends had we met under different circumstances, but watching him under the intense pressure he puts on himself isn't much fun. He realizes this isn't a ball we'd ever find and takes enough time to convince himself it is truly gone, and then declares it lost. Max rolls his eyes at me and we head out to our own balls. I love the game of golf. There is integrity in people, even during the worst playing situations, and all-in-all, Dustin is very professional about the rules of the game.

Max looks long and hard at his third shot. He hits a wedge, and I think I might have tried to hit an easy nine iron in his situation. But he hits it well, and the ball lands ten feet right of the pin and spins back toward it and the front of the green. He'll have a chance for snaking in a birdie.

My shot is just what I wanted; 72 yards straight ahead. The 64-degree lob wedge I've been playing with the last few years has become the favorite club in my bag. I can hit it 80 yards, but 75 is perfect. I feel good about the shot. I hit it pretty well, maybe a touch fat, but it will still have enough on it to make the front of the green and leave me a chance for birdie. My ball is on-line with the pin, but I can now see it is going to be short, perhaps just in front of the green. It comes back to earth, lands about two feet short of the green, and hits a sprinkler head. The ball goes a good thirty feet back into the air and there is a moment where I can only see the ball going up. It appears to be coming back toward the creek. I have my first uneasy feeling of the day. It's amazing how quickly your body can react to an initial sign of trouble. My stomach leaps into my throat and I can feel my pupils dilate. As it comes back to the ground for the second time, my heart skips a beat and my stomach drops right back to its normal position. The ball hits very close to the same sprinkler head and hops just forward enough to catch the fringe of the green. I let out a huge sigh of relief. I will have a putt for another birdie and not be chipping from in front of the creek.

Max turns to me and says, "You're one lucky son of a bitch!"

I couldn't have put it better myself. I've had a charmed life, and I wouldn't change anything except those two hours back in Memphis waiting in the hotel lobby for Sammy. I sometimes dream about how life would have been if she had showed up. I can see my life as being similar, but married with a few kids, still playing golf, and having her by my side during all those difficult times in med school. It would have been nice, but life didn't work out that way.

Dustin is now dropping again, but this time from in front of the creek. He drops and will be hitting his sixth shot and can only hope to get up and down for a double bogey. He drops his ball, stands quickly over it, and hits it to the green. He catches it thin and it runs to the middle of the green, leaving him a much longer putt than was necessary. Three putts later, and he marks down a devastating 9. He is all but done at this point, and I half expect him to quit at the turn.

Max is back "in the zone" as he lines up his putt. He has his game face on and I know he will make this putt. It's uphill, which can break either way if not hit just right. He hits it hard to keep it from falling off to either side, and it hits the back of the cup, bounces straight up, and comes straight down into the bottom of the cup for a great birdie.

My shot is from the fringe of the green. This is technically the first green I've missed today, but being just on the fringe is as good as being on the green, in this situation. My putt, too, is uphill, but there's not much of a break and I know I will have a chance as long as I get it started on the right line. The fringe can have the ability to kick it off-line, as the grass is slightly higher than the grass on the green, but I study it closely and feel it is smooth enough to putt. I make a good stroke, keep my head still, and it drops into the cup one more time!

Hole #9

Par 4 – 498 yards

Max and I wink at each other coming off the 8th green. We don't dare say anything, since Dustin isn't having the best game and we know the golf gods can strike retribution at any time. We've all been there, and we know enough not to celebrate our birdies when someone else has a horrible hole. It isn't right, and we move on like nothing happened. I want to tell Max more about Cindy and what I learned about her mother, but we keep quiet. I tee it up on number 9 and think about the shot at hand. The 9th is a very long hole, usually downwind, and if you get your drive up past the trees, you can catch some of that wind and ride the fairway to the crest of a hill some 275 yards away. After that, the hole slopes downhill toward a lower green. If you don't reach the downhill, you will be staring at a three or five wood into a tight green; but if you make the hill, you can have as little as an eight iron. The winds are favorable today. I only remember playing this hole once where the winds *weren't* favorable. It was the first year of this event. The wind was blowing straight in my face, and it took me three shots to reach the green only to three putt for a smooth double bogey. Today, I am able to get the ball high enough, and as it catches the crest of the hill, it is moving pretty fast. I know I will have a good approach for the second shot. Max hits a bomb slightly off-line to the right. I think it will catch the tops of the branches hanging over the fairway, but his ball just misses them and he lands over the crest of the hill. Unfortunately, his ball kicks hard and a little right, coming to rest in the thick rough, which will probably cost him another 30 yards.

Dustin plays it well, hits it hard, and it flies down past my ball. Overall, it is a great shot, especially after making a nine on the last hole. Max and I are off the tee box as Dustin's ball is airborne, and we pick up with Cindy's mother dying in Montreal.

Since her parents disowned her and there wasn't a known father, the baby became the property of the Canadian government and they felt that due to the circumstances, it was best the baby not be raised in the same city—or country, for that matter. Cindy was sent to an adoption agency in Paris where her soon-to-be adopted father had been transferred on business. It appeared he and her mother would be staying there indefinitely, so they decided to put in for adoption. Being Americans working in France, they had a lot of extra paperwork to trudge through, but it paid off in the end. After many months of waiting, they were told there was a baby available to them. She was raised in Paris for the first year of her life, and when her father was offered early retirement, he took it. Her parents felt that Paris wasn't the place they wanted to raise their child any longer. Since there weren't any restrictions on where they could live once the adoption was finalized, they decided to move back to California.

Nothing I had learned linked the Cindy lying in the hospital with the Sammy I had met in Memphis. Rob wasn't able to find any cousins on the East Coast, and he found that Cindy stayed in California for college. Moreover, every important document—from job paperwork to school transcripts—listed her as "Cynthia Molly Smith." There was no hint of an "aka Samantha" or anything like that. I found myself anxious for her to wake up. I wanted to see if she would recognize me. We were both ten years older, but I was convinced I looked very similar; and she certainly did. Yes, we'd both aged a bit, but not unrecognizably. When I looked at her, it was eerily as though she and I had bumped into each other just the other day. There was, of course, still uncertainty as to whether she would fully recover. Would she have any memory issues? And then there was the uncertainty of how she felt about me if this *was* the same girl. Maybe she decided on the way back to the hotel ten years ago that she didn't want to see me again. Maybe something had happened to her phone and it wiped out my number. But then I figured, if she really wanted to, a girl with her looks could have easily tracked me down by sweet talking the front desk clerk at the hotel. Whatever happened on that day might always remain a mystery to me, unless this girl lying in my hospital in a coma had the answers. Only time would tell.

***

"Is it the same girl?" Max asks eagerly.

I look him straight in the eye and say, "Max, I'm eight under par through eight holes. Last time I did this and stopped talking about the woman who had such a profound impact on me, my game went to hell. I'm not finishing this story until the eighteenth hole."

Max looks shocked and says, "I wasn't sure you realized you were eight under, and I was afraid to say anything."

"As long as we keep talking," I tell him, "I know I'll keep playing well."

He nods his approval, and as impatient as he is to hear the results of this story, he now knows he can ride out the round and hear it step by step. This, of course, is exactly what I need.

Max isn't too excited when he sees his ball in the rough, leaving him over 200 yards to the green from a very thick lie. "Great," he sighs and begins trying to figure out how best to advance the ball. I am glad to see him grab his five wood to get aggressive with the shot. I know he feels that if he gets a little lucky, the ball might get enough club on it to make it to the green; and if he hits it poorly, he can still advance it far enough toward the green to leave himself with a chance to get it up and down for par. This is a shot we used to practice a lot in college; choke down a good two inches on a five wood and hit down on the ball, not allowing the grass to grab the head of the club too hard. A five wood has enough loft on it that if you catch enough of the ball on the downswing, it can come out low and hot. If you get it on-line, you'll be surprised how well it'll advance. Sure enough, Max hits it just as I think he will, and he gets the ball going at the green, but it runs out of gas about 20 yards short of the front. I would have been very pleased with that shot from that lie, and Max is.

I have a much easier shot. My drive ran to the bottom of the hill like I expected, and I have a full seven iron left with a routine shot. *"Keep your head in the game and swing the club. Let the rest happen"*, I tell myself. It turns out as well as any shot I've hit today, once again, giving me another great opportunity for birdie and a 27 on the front nine! Dustin has only a nine iron left for his second shot, and he plays a beauty that ends up just inside my ball. He'll have a great chance to go to school on my putt. I hurriedly tell Max a bit more of the story as we walk to the green.

***

The days passed, and Cindy hadn't shown any signs of change. Her bones were healing, and the longer she stayed in a coma, the better her injuries would be once she woke up. She's still going to feel physically lousy, especially at first and the emotional wounds could easily make her suicidal which has been a discussion between the chief of staff and the head of psychiatry at the hospital. I spent more and more time in her room in the ICU, and the doctors and nurses working in her department were all now very interested in why I'd been so involved. I hadn't shared much with them except that I thought I knew her. They all couldn't wait to see her reaction to me, to see what would happen when she came to. When I was alone with her, I would talk to her, ask her questions I knew she couldn't answer, but there was so much I wanted to know. I spoke to her in two different tones while she slept. One was positive she was Samantha and asking her what happened that day in Memphis. The other was the more realistic one, and it was along the lines of me trying to describe what happened to her and how she looked so much like this girl I knew a long time ago. It was just a way to pass the time sitting with her, and I realized I liked being there regardless of who the hell she was.

***

Max seems more relaxed with this story now that he realizes he is in it for the next nine holes. He has a pretty straight-forward chip ahead of him. He studies the green and hits his ball up high, stopping it about ten feet from the hole. It is a good shot, and I feel he can save par from there. My putt is a little further away than his, and I take my time walking around it from both sides so I can get a good read of the green. I find myself really wanting to make this putt and realize "wanting it" isn't the right approach to the shot, I return my thoughts to the present and focus on the line. I have done this once before, but I was nearly delirious the last time I shot a score like this. This putt will break a little from right-to-left, and I get it started on a good line. However, it stops breaking a few feet from the hole and I start to think I misread it. The ball ever so slowly inches toward the hole, and then just barely catches the right-hand lip of the cup, which pulls it hard left. The ball rolls completely around the cup and heads back toward me, but is still turning. It almost does a full 360-degree rotation around the cup and comes to rest on the edge of the hole. I can't believe it. More than half of the ball is actually hanging over the hole. I start walking in disbelief, but I barely make it two steps when the ball quavers slightly and drops into the cup. I stop dead and stare at it, frozen. My heartbeat quickens, and then I hear about a dozen people start clapping.

The ninth hole comes back to the clubhouse, and Dustin's parents must have told a few people what was going on. Joey Henderson and one of his assistants are there, along with a few other people I don't know. I look at Joey and tip my hat, to which he holds his right hand over his right eye and salutes me, which I thoroughly enjoy. I motion to them to be quiet so Dustin and Max can putt in peace. Dustin gets a great read off my ball and takes a straighter line with much more pace. His ball hits the back of the cup and bounces up in the air, but the momentum carries it past the hole and he has to tap in for par. Max manages to make his, and we head to the snack bar between the ninth green and the tenth tee, where everyone is watching from.

All three of us pull out our score cards to tally up the game so far. I've shot an incredible 27, Max has a one-under 35, and Dustin is very disappointed with a 42.

I wave to him as Joey approaches me, shakes my hand, and asks, "Hey, would you mind if I ride alongside your group in a cart on the back nine?"

I look to Max and Dustin, who make no indication that they object to the idea of a tagalong audience. Dustin doesn't seem super thrilled about having more people watching him falter, but he seems determined to show good sportsmanship.

"Not at all, it would be an honor." I smile gratefully at Joey and thankfully at my playing mates. This is a huge compliment to receive from the course pro, and they are both aware of the enormity of my 27 on the front nine.

"How's your protégé doing?" I ask Joey, "looked like he started strong."

"He had it to 4 under but took a triple on 7, made the turn at even par." He tells me.

It dawns on me how good a score that is for anyone regardless of age and Joey is proud of his student.

I grab an energy drink at the snack bar, and Max gets a hot dog—or a "home wrecker," as we used to call them.

"Oh man, I'm starving!" Max says before taking an entirely too large bite. "I didn't get a chance to eat much this morning," he manages to say through the massive amount of mystery meat and bun in his mouth. I chuckle at his attempt to speak and guzzle the first bit of my energy drink.

Dustin doesn't get anything at the snack bar, and instead heads to the tenth tee. We follow closely behind him, eating and drinking as we walk.

As we approach the tee, I look around to see that there are a handful of people standing behind us; Joey and his assistant, Dustin's parents, another girl off to the side who looks very cute in a white dress with her hair pulled back under a wide-brim hat, two guys I don't know, and a local reporter who had been following the radio personality ahead of us but decided mine would turn out to be a much more interesting story. The girl in the hat walks over to stand near Dustin's parents, and I assume she must be his girlfriend. As we prepare to tee-off, a few more people wander over to the group, but I stop paying attention. It's time to get back to playing and dwelling on my muse.

## Hole #10
### Par 3 – 148 yards

This hole is the shortest on the course; a par three over a pond with three large sand bunkers behind the green. This is the signature hole for the course with a truly picturesque setting. The shot, though, is rather demanding. We have a slight crosswind from our left, and it is a great hole for me to hit an easy 8 iron with a little draw, trying to keep it down under the tops of the trees to avoid the prevailing wind but also to hold it against any breeze it faces. From the tee we're looking at a small green surrounded by a deep forest. With fall in full bloom, the landscape is as beautiful as any setting in New England. The leaves have reached their peak and the colors are as bright as I've ever seen. I notice people taking pictures and I'm not sure if they're attempting to capture something special in the game of golf or the fall colors are the reason for the snapping of shots. I find myself staring at the scene and almost forget I'm out here playing golf.

Dustin catches my eye as I step up to tee up my ball and says, "That was a pleasure to watch, Jim."

I nod at him with sincere approval. I know he means it, and I appreciate the compliment, especially since he is struggling to cope with his score on the front. He looks out over the hole and takes a deep breath to calm himself down for a better back nine. I've played in enough golf tournaments where my playing partners would "no talk" me in hopes of psyching me out. It never bothered me, but I again respect Dustin for saying something.

I swing and the ball jumps off my club like it is on a mission. I often replace a ball after nine holes, even if it's in good shape, and I know many tour players change their ball every few holes. However, I feel this ball has been good to me and I want to stay with "him" the rest of the round. At least, I'm hoping he doesn't decide to get lost somewhere on the back nine! My new best friend is heading right toward the pin, just like he's been doing all day long. It hits five feet right and just past the pin. The flight of the ball is moving just a touch from right to left, and it takes one hop forward then spins back left, coming within two feet of the hole. The small crowd begins to clap its approval, and I decide I love having them there.

Max steps up to the tee, looks at me, and says, "We really need to keep this conversation going!" This is his way of making sure I don't start thinking about golf, and I completely agree. Don't let it all go to my head. So far, so good. Max hits a towering nine iron right at the pin and cuts it into the wind to hold it on-line as the wind has suddenly switched from the opposite direction. I can tell the crowd has pumped him up and his adrenaline is flowing fast and hard. His ball flies over the pin, hits hard, and stops dead. It's a great shot, but he has just a bit too much mustard on it, leaving himself a 20-foot putt, but it's still very nicely done. The crowd again applauds and Max tips his hat like a tour pro.

Dustin looks nervous as he starts his pre-shot routine, and he ends up having to step away from the shot, regroup his head, and start over. It is good that he does, and this time he looks more comfortable over the ball. He has a good swing, very tight and compact, a swing that has a lot of money invested in it over the years. He hits the ball right on-line and the shot looks good all the way. It comes down and hits the pin ever so slightly on the left side, and the ball kicks left and long to about thirty-five feet away. It was a bad break; half an inch left and he might have spun it back for a hole-in-one. He just can't get anything to go his way today. The crowd lets out a sigh and then claps for him, as well. He reaches down and grabs his tee from the ground, throws his clubs over his shoulder, and races off to the green in frustration. We follow behind with a handful of spectators on our heels. Joey and his sidekick are in a cart, but everyone else is walking.

"She woke up on day 33," I tell Max as we walk. His eyes widen and he is excited to hear more.

***

I wasn't there when she came to. The nurse on duty called at 2:15 am to tell me. It had been a very long day at the hospital and I was home sound asleep. The ringing of my phone made me jump. It didn't take me long to get dressed and head to the hospital. There were a few different options for me to get some rest later in the morning before reporting for my shift. The doctors all have lockers at the hospital which provides a place to keep supplies, since there have been days we never leave and taking a shower and grabbing a shave can get you through some long shifts.

When I got to the ICU, the nurse met me at the door and said, "She's really upset. She didn't believe us that she's been here over a month in a coma, and the news of her mother was devastating. But we had to tell her. It was the first thing she asked after 'Where am I?'"

I could hear her sobs from the hall, and I was afraid to go in. I walked over to her room and looked at her through the window. I had a lump in my throat that I tried to clear before going in to see her. She looked at me, and I could see her eyes were very puffy with huge tears running down her cheeks. I was the second doctor to see her; the first was the resident on duty, who was currently reading her brainwave activity. He nodded toward me and said to Cindy, "This is Doctor Peters. He is the anesthesiologist who was with you in surgery the day you arrived."

"Hello, Cindy," I said, mustering up my emotions to give her a sympathetic-yet-friendly smile.

She couldn't say anything, she just stared at me. It was obvious she was in severe emotional pain. They had already given her a shot through her I.V. to calm her down, but it wasn't helping much. I asked her to go through

72

some basic motions for me. I wanted her to think I was only there as her doctor and not some kind of stalker. She could move her pinky, which was recovering but created a good amount of pain. Her ribs were obviously still very sore, and she asked me about her other injuries, which we talked about in-depth. The resident said she appeared to have full memory and brain function, and he explained to her that these were always the primary concerns with every comatose patient. She had looked at me enough that if she knew me from before, she would have had sufficient time to realize it by now and she didn't appear to be suffering from amnesia. She didn't show any signs of recognition, and I was convinced immediately that this wasn't Sammy. It would be a while before I would discuss it with her.

***

Joey has pulled his cart around to the back of the green to get a good look at our putts. Dustin is first to go, and he hits a great putt. It hits the top left of the cup but doesn't drop, so he taps in for a par and the applause is there again. I am thoroughly enjoying having people come along for the ride, but I wonder if they will leave as soon as I make a par. I haven't thought about making one until this moment, and I quickly decide not to think about anything but birdies for the rest of the round.

It is now Max's turn. He takes a long look at the putt, studies it, strokes it, and makes another birdie to the cheers around us. My putt is almost a gimme, and although I don't just tap it in, I only give it a quick look to make sure there isn't anything funny going on between my ball and the cup. I take my normal practice putt, step up to the ball, and ram it into the back of the hole. The crowd again makes a lot of noise in appreciation, and it gives me a warm jolt up my spine. I imagine this is how it must feel to play on tour, and it is a very cool sensation! I look back toward the clubhouse to see a few more people

73

walking our way, and two more golf carts getting under way, as well.

Hole #11

Par 4 – 388 yards


The walk from the 10<sup>th</sup> green to the 11<sup>th</sup> tee is through a magnificent trail with a sea of fall covered leaves covering the sky. The forest is thick, which makes for a great backdrop behind the 10<sup>th</sup> green. The clubhouse does numerous weddings every year, and this area is where they shoot the majority of the wedding pictures. It is truly a spectacular setting. The crowd and Joey are ahead of us, Dustin is slightly behind, and Max and I are somewhere in the middle. This is the longest walk between holes on the course, and I take advantage of the time to get back to Cindy.


\*\*\*


I arrived at Cindy's bedside around 3:00 the morning she woke up, and I stayed with her until she fell asleep a couple hours later. There were other doctors and nurses coming and going, running tests, and I'm sure it was exhausting for her. Every now and then, she would start crying and wanted to be left alone, but after a month-long coma, there was a lot of information that needed to be gathered. When she could calm down, she would ask a lot of questions. I tried to answer as many of them as possible, but some we simply couldn't respond to and they didn't really require any comment. They were more the kinds of questions she would have to come to peace with. The "why me" questions were always the hardest to tap dance around. We had learned the driver of the other car wasn't paying attention on the freeway when he pulled into her lane, sending her car into the center barrier. It flipped into the air and hit a pole, effectively destroying the vehicle. The other driver spent two weeks in the hospital, and we were told there would be charges filed; but we didn't have any more information about it. I promised to call the police station in the morning and have someone from the department come to meet with her over the next few days, which she thought was a good idea.

At 5:30 am, I met outside her room with the other doctors and we discussed her awakening. Everyone was very pleased with how well she had physically come out of the coma, but we agreed the emotional scars were going to be harder to heal. The staff psychiatry department had already been called, and they planned to have someone with her as often as needed over the next few days. Unfortunately, there wasn't anyone on-call when she came to, but there had been much conversation between the departments on how to handle her when she awoke. This was standard procedure in the hospital, and the staff did a great job doing everything by-the-book. There was never a good way to tell someone that a loved one has died, it just has to be said. There isn't any way to sugar coat it, nor should there be. All you can do is be ready to offer support for as long as needed. Cindy was still going to be here at least a few more weeks, since she had too many injuries still needing attention, and this way she could get the physical and emotional rehab she would need.

By 6:00 am, I was in the doctor's lounge trying to get some sleep before I had to be in surgery at 7:30. The case was a scheduled stroke patient. We were supposed to go in and relieve some of the pressure in his brain from fluid buildup, but when I arrived at the operating room, I was informed this elderly gentleman suffered another stroke during pre-op and died before they could get him into the O.R. This wasn't that uncommon when working around serious illnesses. We've lost many, and death is something you learn how to deal with very quickly your first year of medical school. My next surgery wasn't scheduled until 11:00, so I decided to go check on Cindy before grabbing more rest. I've learned how to sleep for moments at a time in the hospital. You have to if you're going to survive in this place; otherwise you walk around in a zombie-state the whole time which isn't great for you or your patients.

When I arrived at Cindy's room in the ICU, she wasn't in her bed. The nursing staff had just changed, and there was a very nice young nurse in her room. She told me Cindy wanted to go to the bathroom, and for the first time in over a month, she could get out of bed. There was another nurse in the bathroom with her, since they couldn't allow her to be by herself. Many people coming out of a coma and learning what she had could easily be suicidal, and they weren't taking any chances. Besides that, she also needed someone with her to get her in and out of the wheelchair with her fractured leg still in a large cast. When she came out of the bathroom, she looked much better than she did earlier and gave me a smile. She seemed happy to see someone she recognized, and I knew the sedatives had taken the edge off her depressed state. She gave me another small smile as the nurse rolled her back to her bed. Despite not having had a shower for as long as it had been, she was a beautiful woman.

"How are you feeling?" I asked.

"Like I've been asleep for a month," she said, a hint of that dazzling smile reflecting in her voice.

"I can't imagine why you feel that way," I told her.

Cindy laughed appreciatively, and then sobered slightly. She had lots of questions for me regarding her condition, and I answered her as honestly as I could. We discussed her being able to leave sometime in the future. There were still quite a few tests we needed to do before that could happen, and she would need at least a couple of weeks of physical therapy before she could walk on her own. Even though this wasn't the girl I had thought about for the last ten years, I didn't want her leaving my hospital so quickly.

***

There are even more people than I expected as we arrive at the 11$^{th}$ tee. The radio jockey is now in the crowd and is busily setting up to do some broadcasting. He usually does this at the end of his round from the clubhouse, but he abandoned his round after fourteen holes to come watch our group, and me in particular. This also saves him the embarrassment of turning in a large number, since he was so far over par, anyway. Joey approaches our group and asks if any of us minds the DJ broadcasting to his station and promises we won't be disturbed. They plan to stay at least a hundred yards away at any time he will be talking. I don't have a problem with it, and the other two guys nod in approval. They are obviously playing second fiddle to me, and if it doesn't bother me, they aren't about to complain.

I tee up my ball and let one rip down the middle of the fairway. The hole turns to the right, and my ball doesn't fade as I expect. Instead, it runs through the fairway into the left-hand rough. I only have about a hundred yards left from there, and the rough shouldn't be too difficult to handle. When you're playing well, it's so easy to remain positive and it never crosses my mind that being in the rough might slow me down. Max pumps a drive up the right side of the fairway, hoping to not make the same mistake I did, but he plays it too close to the trees and catches an overhanging branch with enough force that his ball comes down in the right-hand rough. He is only about eighty yards to the pin, but his ball is stymied behind a tree, leaving an impossible shot to the pin. Dustin hits a smooth three wood to the middle of the dogleg, which is the smartest shot of the group.

Many people following our threesome stay close to the radio setup and seem interested in what the DJ is saying. Dustin's parents and the girl in the white dress are all in the crowd hanging close to him. Again, I try to get a good look at her, but her large-brimmed hat hides most of her face. I can see Dustin looking at her, but she never looks back at him. It seems she is afraid to disturb him "at work."

The DJ is on live at the station, which broadcasts from Boston south to Rhode Island and as far north as Manchester, New Hampshire. He is talking 100% about me; after all, I am now 10 under par through 10 holes and have shot

78

a course record 27 on the front nine. He speaks about the event and how it raises money for local charities, and I try to imagine what it sounds like to the everyday people driving in their cars, stuck in traffic, non-golfers wanting to hear their favorite song but instead hearing about some guy playing golf. I'm not sure it makes for great entertainment. But since this isn't CBS sports covering the event, I am excited there is someone there to witness it.

Although he's trying to stay quiet, I can hear him ask the mic, "What is Jim Peters thinking about to keep his head in this game?" Well, that's easy! Max and I are talking about a girl.

***

Cindy was busy the entire day. Everyone in the hospital who had had contact with her was now aware she was awake and wanted to come see her. She was a young, attractive woman who had been asleep in our hospital for over a month, and my interest in her had created even more speculation. They wanted to see her for themselves. Everyone from the O.R. nurses to the chief-of-staff, and even the orderlies, were showing up, which was when the chief put out a notice on the ICU door limiting the number of visitors to required personnel only. Two of the surgeons who helped put Cindy back together had been in to see her to discuss her injuries and the procedures they did during surgery. They told her that they had to induce the coma to keep her brain from swelling too much and causing permanent damage. She didn't seem too upset about that, but instead, she was truly grateful they had saved her life.

I was in and out to see her the rest of that day. I had another surgery to attend to, but I came back as soon as it was over. A third doctor from her surgery was in her room as I showed up. Alex Rogers was the hand surgeon who put her pinky back together. She had broken it in three places, which means it must have gotten tangled in the steering wheel and twisted severely during the accident. Alex spent six hours working on that one finger. Hand surgery is very intricate. There are more bones in the hand than any other part of the body, and being her pinky, it required a tremendous amount of time to set the bones properly. Of all her injuries, this finger and her ribs were causing her the most discomfort. Because she had been in the coma, there hadn't been any need to give her pain medication; but now it was an important part of her life and would be for some time as she learned to manage the physical pain along with the mental stress.

Alex shook my hand in his own classy way when I arrived and began to introduce me to Cindy, but I told him I'd already been to see her today. Alex looked at Cindy and said, "Dr. Peters here was one of the real heroes the day you arrived. His ability to control your level of anesthesia during a seven-hour operation is to be commended, and it was instrumental in keeping you alive during a very difficult period."

I could see Cindy's eyes swell with tears as she looked at me, and it put a lump in my throat. She started to cry and struggled to say how thankful she was to all of us.

Alex is a true gentleman. He handed her some tissues, put his hand on her shoulder, and told her, "We're all so happy you've come out of your coma with flying colors. You've been through so much, and everyone in this hospital wants nothing more than to help you walk out of here soon."

Well, this was true of everyone except for me. It wasn't that I didn't want her to get better as quickly as possible, but I had strange emotions going on inside my body. In the month she was here, I had gone from thinking about Sammy again and how that one night changed my life to wondering if this was going to have the same impact again to discovering and learning about Cindy; and now the possibility of her leaving had me somewhat afraid. But the reality was that she would be here awhile longer, and I knew there would be time.

Cindy gathered her emotions, looked at Alex, and said, "I'm very fortunate to have ended up in your hospital, and I owe my life to all of you. I don't know if I'll ever be able to repay you, but I hope you all realize how much I appreciate what you've done for me."

Alex was in his early fifties and had a twelve-year-old daughter at home, which had fostered in him a tremendous bedside manner, especially for a surgeon, and I was thankful he was there when I arrived to be a comfort to Cindy. He squeezed her good hand and told her to try to relax and get some rest. He said she could have the nurses contact him anytime if she had any problems or questions and he would be there as quickly as possible. She smiled at him with such sincerity; I imagined she gave her father that look a thousand times when she was younger. It made me realize how alone she must feel here in this room with a rotating door of complete strangers.

Alex shook my hand on his way out and said, "You and I need at least one more round on the golf course before the season is over." He looked at Cindy, "One of these days, I'm going to beat this guy. It's a personal challenge!"

She smiled at him and then gave me a glance I took to mean she was glad I was there. I patted him on the back as he walked away and moved closer to her bed. Her eyes were tearing up again, but she wiped them and apologized for being so emotional. I wanted to reach for her hand and assure her it was completely normal to go through this range of emotions considering all she'd been through, but instead I just tried to comfort her with my words. I was afraid she would think something weird of me touching her, so I tried to keep this as professional as I could. Even though Dr. Rogers had just been very physical, his age somehow seemed to allow him to get away with it. I had spent many hours here in her room with her, but she wasn't aware of it and I was very self-conscious of what she was thinking of me.

We talked about the psychiatrist who came to see her earlier that morning. They had talked for a very long time. She told me how she was learning to deal with the death of her mother. Although it had been over a month since she died, to her it had only happened yesterday. I told her that it was going to take time for her to come to peace with it. She nodded and her eyes glistened with tears again. I could tell she really wanted to cry but was just too worn out to do so.

***

I look at Max. It seems like he is about to get emotional on me, so I wink and say, "I told you this was going to be a long story." Then I walk to my ball, put my bag on the ground, and watch him walk toward his.

Dustin is now over his shot and looking very serious. He puts a good move on the ball and throws it high at the pin, but it comes up slightly short and takes a terrible bounce on the collar of the green dead right. He will still have a putt from there, although if his ball landed an inch either direction he would have had a kick-in birdie and he doesn't like the result. I am next to play. I have 108 yards left from another fluffy lie in the rough, which doesn't give me any trouble. I hit an easy choked-down pitching wedge at about eighty percent, which makes the ball come out high and on-line. I just can't do anything wrong. It's like I am throwing darts at the pins. My ball lands softly on the green and rolls toward the hole, stopping less than twelve feet short. The people surrounding the green let out a loud round of applause and, again, I just know I'll make the putt.

Max has a little less than 80 yards to go, but he is behind a tree and in the rough. I can tell his ball isn't sitting up as nice as mine had been. He has to play more of a knock-down bump-and-run, similar to the kind of shot you see played at the British Open, but he can't go straight at the green. He pulls it off well with just a little too much on the seven iron; he hits it and it runs to the right of the green and past the pin a good seventy-five feet. The crowd claps in appreciation, knowing he did better than most of them could have. We all walk up to the green from different angles; I'm left of the fairway, Max was right, and Dustin comes right up the middle. As I walk, I think of Cindy, take in the scenery, and am truly amazed at how large our little crowd has grown. There must be thirty to forty people standing off the green. Joey now has two of his assistant golf pros working the crowd to make sure they don't create any problems for us, and I am impressed how good a job they are doing. As much as I know Joey wishes he was the center of all this attention, he is showing his true colors and doing everything he can to keep his tournament running smoothly.

Max is first to play. He takes his time, and even though he is far behind my score, he plays like he wants to win. He studies his long chip, steps over it, and hits it well. The ball tracks toward the hole but it has a bit too much speed. I watch his ball rolling on the green and try to will the ball to slow down, but it runs a good 15 feet past the pin. Max makes the long walk down the green to the quiet but respectful applause of the crowd and marks his ball. Dustin then putts his ball from the fringe of the green to inside a foot of the pin, walks up, and taps in for par. He nods to the crowd like a tour player and I see him smile for the first time today. Dustin is a nice kid, and I feel he is finally appreciating being there instead of feeling the pressure.

A wave of stress suddenly crashes over me as I look over my putt. *"Get a grip, Jim!"* I tell myself. *"Think about Cindy. Focus on her beautiful smile."* In that short moment as I bend down to study the line of this putt, it dawns on me that my mind has replaced Sammy with Cindy, something I wasn't sure was possible until this very moment. It is like I am all alone out here without anyone watching me. I slowly stand up, look at the ball, think of Cindy, look at the hole, look back at the ball, make my stroke, and by the time I look up, the ball is nestled into the hole. Everyone cheers and I come out of my glorious ten-second dream. All I can do is smile.

Hole #12

Par 4 – 412 yards

Walking to the twelfth hole, I have plenty of time to tell Max more about Cindy's story.

***

I had left Cindy with the promise I'd be back the next day. All I wanted to do was go home, take a long shower, and get some sleep. I was physically and emotionally exhausted, and my body was telling me to rest. I went to the locker room to change from my scrubs to my normal clothes and was almost out the door to my car when David Johnson from security paged me. His office wasn't far from where I was, so I quickly went to see him. I entered his security room and was greeted by the usual sight of a collection of video monitors, two men watching them, and a girl working on a computer at a desk in the corner. There were no windows in this room, and I was glad I didn't have to sit there eight hours a day.

Dave waved me into his office in the back. He was sitting at his desk and there was a window looking out toward the employee parking lot. He told me to take a seat across the desk from him.

"Jim, I've finally received some information from the adoption agency in Paris, which shed some light on this case. It turns out Cynthia Smith was born to Crystal Wadel in Canada. Crystal was a young unwed girl of eighteen and died during the delivery."

"I know that already," I told him, slightly put out at this repetition of information.

"Yeah, but there's more," he said. "Your buddy Rob called me today, and after doing some digging around, he discovered something that'll shock the

84

hell out of you."

I was too tired to imagine what he could possibly tell me that could shock me any further, so I contented myself with staring blankly at him.

"Rob wanted to talk to you himself when he called, but you were in surgery and he was heading to catch a plane." Then he asked me, "What was the date you last saw Samantha in Memphis?"

I didn't have the slightest notion what that had to do with Cindy, but I answered automatically since that date has been ingrained in my head, "May 14th."

His next words hit me like a ton of bricks. "Crystal Wadel gave birth to twins. Cynthia Smith and Samantha Lang are identical twin sisters. Samantha Lang is the girl you met in Memphis."

"WHAT?" I screamed. "Are you fucking serious? How? When? How the hell did you find this out?" I was shaking. Could it really be true? I had managed to meet these identical twin sisters ten years apart?

"Jim." David was now coming around his desk to calm me down. He put his hand on my shoulder to keep me in my chair. "Samantha Lang died in a car crash May 14th in Memphis ten years ago, most likely on her way to meet you."

I felt like I was going to be sick. "How do you know that? How can you be sure, Dave? This is some heavy shit you're telling me. How do you know it's accurate?" I wasn't really asking him; it was more like I was yelling at him. I noticed he was looking out the front of his office to see if his staff was seeing my emotional outburst. I took a few deep breaths, trying to calm down.

"Rob found this out in the last twenty-four hours. He flew down to Memphis to meet with Samantha's cousin this afternoon. He wants to talk to you as soon as he lands, but he wanted me to tell you this first. Give you a heads up."

\*\*\*

Max is stunned as I tell him this. I step away from him and tee up my ball. "Un-fucking-believable, huh?" I say to him quietly enough that nobody else can hear. He looks pale and confused. I then glance at Dustin, who has no idea what we are talking about but is looking like he wants to get in on this conversation. I have to step away from the shot, regroup, look down the fairway, set the tempo in my head, and swing my club, which feels like it is an extension of my body. My shoulders turn, my arms follow, and as smoothly as I've ever felt it, the ball jumps off my club with force and power, splitting the fairway in two.

"She died on her way to meet me at the hotel," I whisper to him as he steps up to the tee.

"Unreal," he says, and still looking like he's seen a ghost, he sets up for his shot. Under normal conditions, this would have shaken another golfer, but I know Max won't alter from his game while digesting this information. Although I know he feels this blow nearly as acutely as I did, he keeps it together and rips his ball down the fairway.

"What the hell are the two of you talking about?" Dustin asks as he takes the tee.

"Just telling him a story about an old girlfriend," I tell him.

"Must have been some girl," he says and proceeds to hit his best drive of the day.

"Nice shot! And yes, she was." I smile at Dustin as Max and I grab our bags and head off the tee. "I was on a plane that night to Memphis to meet Rob," I tell Max.

\*\*\*

86

I was able to get out of a morning surgery the next day, and since I had the next afternoon and following day off, I had to go. Rob and I talked on the phone when he landed, and I had already packed an overnight bag and was on my way to the airport. He knew I would come and he had almost made me a reservation, but not knowing my schedule, he decided to go on ahead and figured I'd come as soon as I could. Rob rented a car, met with Sammy's cousin, and then came back to pick me up when my flight came in.

As soon as I was in the car, Rob started recounting all the new information he had obtained. He had discovered that Sammy and Cindy were born in Montreal, and due to the untimely death of their mother during the birth, with no father on record and their grandparents had already disowned their mother, so the hospital turned the girls over to the adoption agency in Montreal. Due to the local press the story had received, the agency felt better sending the girls to different countries in the hope that they could each have a fresh start at a normal life. Canadian law didn't require the twins stay together, and separating them seemed to make perfect sense at the time. Cindy went to Paris and Sammy to Atlanta, where she was adopted by a couple in their 30's. They were a nice family. Her parents were unable to have a child of their own, and when the local agency in Atlanta contacted them saying there was a newborn in Canada they could adopt immediately, they jumped at the chance. Sammy was flown to Atlanta, where she was raised by wonderful parents. The father had a sister, Wendy's mother, who was divorced, and her father wasn't ever in the picture after Wendy was eighteen months old. Wendy and Sammy were very close growing up and lived near each other in Atlanta until Wendy's mother was given a great job offer and moved with the then fifteen-year-old Wendy to Memphis. Sammy and Wendy got together as often as possible after the move, and Sammy was just about to finish her freshman year at Atlanta University when she met me.

Wendy was uncertain about meeting with Rob when he first called, but when he mentioned my name, she agreed. Rob found that Wendy remembered the day Sammy told her about me like it was yesterday. She explained how they found her car and Sammy took off to meet her "prince charming." She had a little time before she was supposed to meet me at 3:00, so she was going for a drive outside the city to get some fresh air. Sammy loved her car and taking long rides with the music cranked up, which was why she enjoyed driving from Atlanta to Memphis to visit her only cousin.

***

The 12$^{th}$ hole is very routine. All three of us hit the fairway, and that is quickly followed by all three of us hitting the green. The crowd applauds and I continue telling Max how Rob and I pieced all the details together while we walk from the tee to the fairway and from the fairway to the green.

***

It was like we were playing out a spy story, and although it was very emotional for me, I got more excited the more I learned. I was incredibly grateful for all Rob's help. He had chosen to fly down there on his own nickel as a favor to me, and it now appeared he was almost as interested in seeing how this all played out as I was. I might have been able to do it alone, but having him there made the whole operation much smoother than if I'd been on my own. He was more interested on an intellectual level, and I was more emotionally attached, which doesn't always make for a good situation when you're trying to find information, so Rob led the charge. We left the airport to go see Wendy, who was anxious to finally meet me. I hadn't realized the impact Sammy's death had had on her. I guess I was too selfish with my own grief that I overlooked others were hurt, as well, and some much more than me. The

88

difference was that I had just learned she had died in the last few hours, whereas her family has had ten years to come to peace with it.

When we arrived at Wendy's house, it was after 10:00 pm. She opened the door and simply couldn't talk. Wendy was an attractive woman. She was thirty years old, a year older than Sammy would have been. Her home was typical of a Memphis suburb. It was obvious they didn't live in luxury, but I didn't get the impression that they were in any financial trouble. It turned out that she was married with two small children. She worked at the daycare center they went to, and her husband was a mechanic at a local garage in Memphis. She covered her mouth as she looked at me and started to cry. I seemed to have that effect on women recently. She excused herself and her husband came outside. He introduced himself as Steve and explained that this had been a very emotional day for his wife. Rob hadn't mentioned Cindy yet. He had only said I'd contacted him to help locate Samantha, and that he'd only had any luck doing so in the last month. Samantha's parents were still in Atlanta, but the Wendy connection seemed like it would produce more answers, which is why Rob came here first.

Steve was very jovial. He eagerly told us how he had heard about me from the time he met Wendy eight years ago. They'd been married six years, and the kids were two and four years old. They were sleeping now, but they had been a little confused why mommy was so upset when they went to bed. Steve invited us in and asked if he could get us anything. We politely declined; this wasn't a time to eat or drink. Wendy came back into the room and walked up to me to shake my hand and apologize for her behavior. I assured her that wasn't necessary in the slightest. I had ten years of emotions built up inside me, and I wasn't sure how long it would be before I broke down. She was a very nice woman and I could only imagine how close she and Sammy had been. I didn't have much to go on, though. During the night I had spent with Sammy, we didn't have much time to talk about other people. I knew vaguely about her cousin, but that was it.

Wendy urged me to tell my story first, and I felt obligated to do so. I started from the beginning and didn't leave out any details. It took me the better part of an hour to get through it, and at times I had to pause before getting too emotional. She also got choked up as I talked, and I tried to lighten up the narrative as I saw it get difficult for her. Rob and Steve didn't say anything, but they hung onto every word like they were going to be reporting a story on it. I ended with getting through medical school and left it at how I was now working as a doctor in Boston. Rob added that research he was doing on another adoption had led him to Samantha. We decided not to tell Wendy about Cindy just yet. I knew I would before the night was over, but I wanted to get through Wendy's story before I sprang it on her that she had another relative in a hospital bed in Boston.

It was well after 11:00 when Wendy started in on everything Sammy had told her ten years ago on that early morning when she returned home by cab. Everything she knew about me was pretty much word-for-word what I had told Sammy. She said she remembered it because she had played it over and over in her head a thousand times after Sammy's death, but she never thought to look for me because she didn't have enough information. Sammy couldn't remember the name of the hotel, and she only referred to me as "Jim." Her search for me would have been even more futile than mine for Sammy. Although Wendy's story of the night Sammy and I spent together was identical to mine, she had a lot more to tell me about Sammy. I didn't know very much about her, her parents, her college, or her friends. There was so much I didn't know, and Wendy was slowly filling in the blanks to the questions I had thought about repeatedly over the last ten years. When we got up to the time Sammy left me in the cab, Wendy filled in the details piece by piece.

Sammy had called Wendy from the cab, telling her she would be home shortly. Wendy was asleep and a little worried, but not too much so as she always knew Sammy would be fine. She got up and waited for her to arrive. She said Sammy came in grinning from ear to ear.

"It must have been some movie?" Wendy said.

Sammy immediately stated that she had met the man of her dreams and proceeded to tell her every detail of the night spent with "Jimmy." Nobody ever called me that, not even Sammy while we were together that night, but apparently, she liked it by the time she began telling Wendy about me. Wendy explained how they sat at the kitchen table in her little apartment, having breakfast and going through the night. Sammy was exhausted but unwilling to sleep, so they talked for hours before both took a quick nap. Wendy woke her up at noon and Sammy jumped in the shower to clean up and go run errands with Wendy before they went to look for her car. They thought they might need some extra time to look for it, since we had been so unsuccessful the night before, but they found it in less than ten minutes. In our defense, we were walking around in the dark and they were driving in broad daylight. When they got to her car, Sammy took everything out of Wendy's car in preparation for driving back to Atlanta after I left. She promised to call Wendy once she was on her way and said she would tell her all about our afternoon together.

Wendy gave me a steady look. "She was head-over-heels for you. If you had asked her to marry you that day, she would have said yes and followed you anywhere." As she said those words I felt the blood rush through my body and my face must have shown it but my mind couldn't produce any coherent words, so Wendy continued her story.

What happened next was where the mystery began. Sammy told her since she had some time to waste, she was going for a ride in the country before heading back to meet me in the city. Sammy had sent me two text messages and talked to Wendy twice between 1:00 and roughly 2:30, then she disappeared. She apparently lost control of her car shortly after sending me a text at 2:36. I still had it in my phone, since I was careful to forward it every time I got a new phone. I showed it to Wendy; the picture of Sammy in the car smiling sexily at me with text saying, "c u soon." I'd looked at that picture a million times. Wendy suppressed a sob as she saw the image and had to take a moment before she could go on.

Because Wendy had to work that afternoon and evening, she didn't get too worried about Sammy. She figured I probably stayed to catch a later flight and we were still hanging out. It wasn't until later that night after not being able to reach her that Wendy called the police and her parents in Atlanta. There wasn't even a search until a few days later, but nothing came of it initially. They weren't looking for me because they didn't have any information, just some guy named Jim. Sammy had forgotten to mention I was in town for a golf tournament, so they didn't have anything to go on. She was considered a missing person until one day a couple of kids playing in the river found her car. They didn't even know someone was inside it until they hauled it out of the water. That's when all hell broke loose. Her parents had hired private investigators during that month and they too came up empty handed. The police ruled it an accident and concluded she was distracted by her phone, possibly text messaging since they found her phone stuck in her hand but it had been destroyed in the water during the month she was there. They were unable to retrieve any information from the phone. It became sickeningly obvious that last text message to me may have been what took her life. Wendy must have seen the sudden guilt and anguish on my face because she assured me that I couldn't take the blame. Sammy was always on her phone. Still, it was all very disturbing to me.

Samantha's car ran off that country road along a river and the car was submerged deep in the mud below the water. The gravel alongside the road didn't leave any tire marks where she veered into the river, and since nobody saw her or knew exactly where she was, the search had been impossible. If those kids hadn't been playing in the water at that exact spot, she might still be missing.

Wendy then asked Rob to clarify how he was able to put this all together. We looked at each other. The rest of this conversation was going to make Wendy even more upset, but it had to be said. I said I would take this one and proceeded to explain what happened when Cynthia arrived in our hospital a little more than a month ago. I told her everything and didn't leave anything out, leading right up to me sitting there with her at that moment. Wendy and Steve were floored. They couldn't believe there was an identical twin to Samantha in a hospital bed who had been struggling to survive. And then they realized the impact this would have on Sammy's adopted parents—Wendy's aunt and uncle. She had grown apart from them after they found Sammy's body. Wendy felt somewhat responsible, and though they never blamed her for losing their daughter, Sammy was their entire life. They made every sacrifice possible to give Sammy a charmed life, and she was their perfect daughter. It just became too hard to be around them.

Wendy was now in tears again, and Steve went to comfort her. If I had been alone, I'm sure I would have been crying, as well, but being with them caused me to put my doctor face on. I'd been on the side of giving bad news for so long that I had become numb to it, and I was relying on that strong force of habit to hold it together.

Once she could speak, Wendy stated, "I have to go to Atlanta."

Rob replied, "Jim and I are booked on the first flight in the morning, actually."

"I'm coming with you." Wendy's expression said plainly that she wouldn't be denied this, as though either Rob or I would ever dream of telling her she wasn't allowed to come with."

I realized then how difficult meeting Sammy's parents was going to be, but there wasn't any way I couldn't go. It had to be done, and they needed to know.

Wendy seemed to be able to read my mind. "Jim, they never blamed you for what happened. Sammy was living her life to the fullest, and that was all they ever wanted for her."

It was well after midnight when Rob and I made arrangements to meet Wendy at the airport in the morning, and we left to find a hotel and get some rest. Tomorrow was going to be another long day. It seemed like a long time ago I was in the room with Cindy, but it was only that morning. My life seemed to have these lengthy days, no matter what I did.

***

"Holy crap," Max says as he just misses his putt for birdie.

"That's one way of putting it," I respond, then grow quiet so Max can putt out. We both remain silent as Dustin taps in for birdie. The swelling crowd claps appreciatively at the high level of golf they're witnessing.

I step up to my ball and Max says flatly, "That is some seriously heavy shit."

"Isn't it?" I make my stroke and the ball falls safely into the cup. Another birdie on my quest for 54!

Hole #13

Par 4 – 452 yards

Max is nearly in shock at this point in the story. "How could you have done all this without me knowing about it?"

"It all happened so fast in just the past couple weeks," I tell him. "I didn't have the energy to go through it while it was going on. Besides," I say teasingly, "it appears you've had your hands full with Vanessa, who *you* hadn't said one word about."

He laughs. "Fair enough." As I think about Vanessa again, that image of her standing naked at the pool during the earthquake manifests vividly in my head. I really hope I get to meet her someday.

I pause for a brief moment thinking about Vanessa as I get ready to hit my next tee shot. This is the hardest tee shot on the course, and the thought of this beautiful redhead is just the image I need to get me to relax into the shot. I am keenly aware how realistic the 54 Watch is now, otherwise there wouldn't be so many people hanging around. This hole is long, and the tee shot has to carry over 250 yards downhill but stop before the fairway runs out at 280 yards. It is a bit like hitting a driver to a green only to leave you a long iron uphill to another, very small green. I've birdied this hole before, but I've also made some big numbers. The shot requires a good drive and so far today all the other tee shots have seemed to work easily, but I know this will take a lot of skill to position myself for another birdie opportunity, and I have confidence I can do it. I tee my ball up slightly higher than normal to get a good launch angle so I can hit it high and stop it quickly. I give the shot its proper due, then clear my head, put a nice image of Vanessa there just long enough to relax, clear that thought, turn my shoulders, and let it fly.

The ball comes off my club lower than I expected and I immediately start talking to my ball. "Sit down, sit down. Easy. Easy. Hold on!" However, it ignores everything I say to it, and I can see it heading for the ravine at the end of the fairway. It hits just short of the rough, takes a hop forward, and I gasp, knowing it's gone too far. As the ball hits the first cut of rough, it slows down a bit, and then trickles into the very beginning of the hazard. There is a loud moan from the crowd, and I figure I have a 50-50 chance at a shot if I didn't lose the ball completely. Just then, Dustin's parents start motioning with their arms like an umpire calling a runner safe in baseball, and the girl in the white dress is clapping feverishly. I relax, thinking I'll have a shot, and then it dawns on me that Dustin might be upset with them for being so supportive of me. I glance in his direction and he smiles back at me. It is the first time today I realize he is actually rooting for me. It is like he's playing for the other team in a no-hitter: he wants to win, but at the same time he knows he's watching something special. I smile back at him approvingly and my heart begins to slowly return to a less stressful beat.

Dustin is next and he grabs a 3 wood, which is probably the safer play. He isn't going to make the same mistake I did. He hits a good shot, but it has too much hook-spin on it and it dives quickly toward the backside of the water. He bends his whole body to the right, trying to will the ball out of the water in a gesture that every golfer has made at one time or another. It doesn't really help, but it just seems like the thing to do, and the harder you lean, the worse the shot you just hit. By the looks of it, Dustin didn't make the shot he wanted to. We watch for what seems like a long time, waiting for it to land, and when it finally comes back to earth, we see a small splash followed by his ball flying straight back up into the air. It must have hit a rock toward the end of the water hazard, and it looks like it might go forward just enough to get him over. However, it comes down just past the water's edge and sinks deep into the mud. He looks at me with his shoulder up, hoping either Max or I have some good news for him.

"It looks like it's in the mud," I say, "but you might still have a shot."

Max agrees, but you can see Dustin slump with the thought of his next shot. Max slowly takes the tee. He isn't anxious to follow that shot. He goes back to his bag and grabs a driver. I figure he will try to hit it similar to mine, but take a little off. He aims toward the large tree on the right side of the end of the fairway which confuses me as he will have to draw it away from that tree. That will make his ball fly a little farther and can put him in trouble, but I imagine he is just going to swing it easier and move it away from the tree. He tees it high and draws his club backward. I expect him to make a smooth, easy swing and make sure he gets it in the fairway, but as he starts his downswing, he goes after it like this is a long drive contest. I never thought of trying to fly the ravine, but Max decides this is the time to go for it! His ball takes off with enormous velocity. He starts it just left of the big tree, and it doesn't move one inch left or right. He will need to carry it over 300 yards to clear the ditch, but it's all downhill and, as I now notice, the wind is ever so slightly behind us. He later tells me once he felt that breeze switch from the normal in-our-face on this hole to that slight tail wind, he thought he could get over.

It is an incredible shot. The ball misses the tree by inches, clears the ditch, and finds the fairway on the other side. The crowd goes crazy. Most of the people watching are serious golfers, and know how hard that shot is to pull off and understands the talent required to make it. I look at him in utter amazement. We've played this course together a number of times and never have I seen him even attempt anything like that. Max just grins and says, "I still have a few tricks left in this bag, Old Man!"

I laugh and we all grab our bags to walk off the tee together. It seems like Dustin wants to hang with us for the first time today, and of course Max and I have a story to get back to, but we engage him when he looks at Max and says, "That was one hell of a shot!"

"Thanks, Dustin." Max says with true sincerity.

I ask him, "What gave you the balls to go for that shot now?"

Max just grins and says simply, "I can't let you steal all the thunder out here, Mr. 54."

With that, I know we have to get our conversation back to a girl or that 54 will slip away like a thief in the night. Although I want to get back to my story, I figure it is best to bring Vanessa up with Dustin around. The Cindy story is too deep for someone to unknowingly walk into. "So, do I get to meet this mysterious Vanessa chick, or are you hiding her away in some cabin in the woods?" I ask nonchalantly.

Max gives me another grin. "She's actually here today."

"Really?" I ask in amazement.

"Yep. You'll meet her after the round."

We didn't say another word until we reach Dustin's ball, which I think is probably odd for Dustin since Max and I haven't stopped talking all day. The thought of actually meeting this cute little redhead gives me something to ponder, and I just can't find the words to summarize all the thoughts going through my head. I always knew Max would eventually fall hard for a girl, but I wasn't expecting that he'd done it in the past few months. I look at Dustin and it appears to me he is just happy being able to be included in our group. He is so far behind me, the thoughts of him winning today are long gone and he is finding peace with his round of golf. I know he is enjoying himself without having to have any conversation. It is a pretty cool experience to be the center of attention out here, the three of us just walking along while the growing crowd watches our every move.

We find Dustin's ball in the hazard. It apparently hit the mud and rolled 3 inches away. That might not seem like much, but those 3 inches made the difference between dropping out of the mud with a one stroke penalty or being able to get a club on it and advancing it toward the green. He stands in the hazard, his right foot slightly in the water and his left literally stuck in the mud. His ball is a mess and barely any white can be seen through all the dark mud coating it. Since he has a shot, he knows it's the right play. He could have gone back on the other side of the pond, cleaned his ball, taken the penalty stroke, and had a long shot to the uphill green. I would have played the mud ball, too. Dustin has at least 200 yards to the pin. Mud can really affect the ball flight, and there are entire books devoted to how best to play the mud ball. But it's been my experience that you just have to go after it, hit it clean (no pun intended), and hope the force of the shot knocks as much grime off the ball as possible. The shot requires a hard-struck long iron, maybe a 4 or even a 3 iron, but because he has to get it up over the lip of the hazard only a few feet in front of him, he probably can only hit a 7 iron, maybe a 6. Knowing he won't reach the green, he takes an 8 iron to make sure he just puts it in play over the ditch and gives himself a chance to get up and down for par. He settles in over the shot and makes a hard descending blow to the ball, shooting it up high over the lip and heading to safety in the fairway up ahead. Mud splatters Dustin, coating everything from the ankles of his pristine white pants right on up to his face. The crowd once again erupts with cheers. Dustin grabs his towel and tries in vain to clean himself off, but it quickly becomes apparent the endeavor is hopeless. The more he tries to wipe the mud away, the dirtier he gets. Finally, he burst out in laughter at the futility of his efforts and settles for simply wiping off his face as best he can. Max and I chuckle, too, since that is all any of us can do. I can hear the DJ boasting about it on the air. Although it is completely appropriate, Joey quiets him down.

I have my own problems up ahead. My ball has settled into the tall grass, and I would have been lucky to find it if the spectators hadn't showed me exactly where it was. The grass is just thin enough for me to have a shot. Had it been another foot forward, I would be dropping and hitting three, all but certain to end this birdie streak I am so enjoying. This was big. It was bigger than I had allowed myself to realize, and I still refuse to give it too much thought. I learned not to do that a decade ago. *See the shot, make the swing, and don't think about trying to make another birdie! Stay in the moment and deal with what is right in front of you.* This is the first shot today I've needed to calm myself down before swinging, and I know I can pull it off. I'm not going to let a little tall grass slow me down. I look at Max, who is not nearly as confident I can pull this shot off as I am, and I can see it in his face; he is pulling for me and he wants me to do what's never been done before. The dream of 54 has always been a possibility for every golfer who has stood on the first tee of every round ever played, but doing it has never happened.

"Today?" I say to him, and he knows exactly what I mean. Would I meet Vanessa today?

"Absolutely," he replies. He smiles, realizing my thought of Vanessa is right on track. I've given the shot at hand its proper due, cleared my head, thought of a beautiful girl, and am ready to swing the club. I have 174 yards uphill to the pin. I choke down on my 6 iron just a bit to make sure not to hit the shot fat, swing well, and the ball comes out perfectly, heading to the flag. I know I didn't get 100% of it and I am worried it will catch the bunker guarding the front of the green, so I yell for it to get up. It does, just clears the bunker, and makes it to the green. I have my longest putt of the day coming up now, but at least it is directly into the hill and perfectly straight. All I need to do is get it started on the right line and give it enough speed to get there, and I'll have a good chance.

I have a brief moment of doubt when I approach the green and see the actual distance of the putt. The idea of missing the putt is my first negative thought of the day, and unlike ten years ago when I allowed those thoughts to remain in my head, I have learned how to appreciate the negative thought and remove it. I visualize a little man inside my head taking the "bad" thought and walking it right out of one of my ears. This is a little game Jack helped me develop in college, and we used to spend hours talking about it. I make a mental note to discuss this very moment with him later. I have the little man remove the negative thought and I easily replace it with Cindy; the image of the day I saw her full face when they removed her bandages is as fresh as ever. She was so beautiful. Although memories of that day bring back hordes of confusing memories and emotions, it is also a memory I revisit all the time when I need a boost.

I walk ahead of Max off the right side of the fairway to not disturb him, and the farther right I walk, the easier it is for me to see my upcoming putt; it's really not as bad as I have been letting myself think. His drive has left him a short shot to the green. I imagine many others have driven their ball over that ravine in the past, but I have serious doubts anyone had ever done it from the back tees during a tournament of this level. I've had this shot before, but it was never a second shot on this hole. I've had times I was in the hazard and had to lay up to this point in hopes of getting up and down for par, but to have this opportunity to get up and down for birdie was incredible. With his uphill lie, Max is able to loft the ball almost straight up, high above the pin, with a towering wedge shot. I think the ball is actually still climbing as it rises above the green, and it seems like it has eyes as it reaches its pinnacle high over the green. It takes dead aim at the pin and drops straight down at the hole. From my vantage point, I can tell it will be very close, and it is. The ball drops right next to the pin, makes one small hop an inch from where it hit, and stops dead 18 inches from the hole. It is an incredible shot, and the roar of the crowd can probably be heard back at the clubhouse. Max looks questioningly at me, voicelessly asking if the ball dropped into the cup. The noise is so loud, he apparently thinks maybe it went in. I hold my hands up to show him the distance like I was describing a large trout I'd caught. He raises his club in appreciation and gives a large smile. This really is fun out here!

Dustin is next to play. His ball is still pretty dirty and he has about 100 yards still to negotiate. There is enough mud to create some problems with his ball flight, and it is a shot needing a little luck if he is going to save par. He hits a hard gap wedge, again hoping to rid the ball of the rest of the mud and thinking he can hit it high up the hill to allow it to find the green. The shot comes off too low and goes deep into the green, settling two inches off the green in the first cut of the fringe. This is a shame, as now he won't be able to clean his ball since he isn't technically on the green, and the large piece of mud still directly on top of his ball is going to make a huge impact on the roll of his putt. The gentle applause makes him believe he is on the green and he doesn't realize the enormity of the penalty he will be facing by missing the green by those last couple of inches; but as he approaches the ball, it becomes painfully obvious. Dustin and I are at opposite sides of the green but he is just off and will be first to play. Max goes up to mark his ball and fix his divot as I mark my ball and wipe it with the wet towel I keep on my bag. I dipped the towel in the pond while I was there a few moments ago. I wet half my towel down at least two or three times a round to keep it damp. As much as my putt is uphill and straight, Dustin's is downhill and has an early left-to-right break, but the mud will be the real issue. He starts the ball on a good line, but with every rotation, it hops in the air and looks like Cyclops tumbling down a hill. The crowd is cheering and laughing at the same time. It is quite entertaining watching this lumpy little ball rolling toward the cup, but every time the mud reappears, it seems to move the ball in a different direction. By the time it comes to a stop, he has about 10 feet left to the hole, still slightly above it but off-line to the right. I think Dustin did a great job under the circumstances, and everyone is supportive of his effort.

My turn. I have at least 30 feet left to keep this streak going. I like the line, and the hole being uphill gives me the chance to put a firm stroke on the ball. I stay in the moment and commit to the putt, but I hit it a tad too hard and it jumps off my putter with more authority than I had hoped. I don't move as it tracks towards the cup. "Slow down, slow down!" I mutter at the ball, trying hard to keep it under my breath. The ball slams into the back of the cup, jumps straight up into the air, hits the ground above the hole, and comes to rest just outside the cup for almost a second before dropping in. Again, I go through a range of emotions in that split second the ball sat above the cup and I had this vision of it staying there but thankfully it fell back into the hole.

The crowd is absolutely going crazy, jumping up and down; the DJ shouts unabashedly into his microphone, all thoughts of remaining respectfully quiet forgotten; and the reporter scribbles like mad, somehow magically not destroying his notepad with his pen. Although wanting to jump around and act like an excited five-year-old in my moment of euphoria, I settle instead on taking off my hat and waving it modestly in the air. Both Max and Dustin come up and give me high-fives, but Max holds onto my hand and throws his arm around my shoulder to give me a squeeze. I am as happy in that moment as I have ever been in my life, and once again I think about Cindy. I wish she was here to see this!

I notice Joey standing off the green, his golf cart parked beyond the trees behind him. He has his arms crossed over his chest and is staring at me, shaking his head and grinning. I reach down and pick my ball from the hole. I hold it over my head, and again, the crowd cheers. I put my hat back on my head and attempt to calm everyone down so Dustin can take his shot. It takes a moment, but things finally settle down and Dustin looks over his 10-footer for bogey. He makes a good stroke, but the freshly cleaned ball refuses to drop, coming to rest inches from the cup. He taps in for a 6, and the crowd claps lightly, giving their approval of what turned out to be a very difficult hole for him. Max taps in without a thought, the crowd claps again, and we all move toward the 14th hole. He looks at me and says, "That was very Seve like of you!" referring to the late great professional golfer Severino Ballesteros who could make birdie better than anyone from the most difficult situations and I'm reminded how I grew up watching Seve play some of the most spectacular shots I've ever seen. I'm honored for the comparison.

Time for my story is now running out, and I am insistent on telling it all to Max before we finish the round. This excitement of this hole took some of

103

the storytelling time away, and as we walk to the next tee, I look at Max and he says, "We have to get back to Atlanta."

Hole #14

Par 4 – 395 yards

Amid all the commotion, Joey is doing a good job with keeping everyone moving and away from us. There aren't any ropes separating the players and the spectators like in a PGA tour event, but the people are very respectful and walking fast to get ahead of us. Joey tells us to slow down and he'll move everyone up the fairway and away from the tee box. Most people prefer to be ahead on the tee shot, anyway. There are now a handful of other people in golf carts driving up from the clubhouse. Since this is a walking tournament, they are apparently allowing guests and finished players to use them to catch up with us. The beer cart is also hanging around; Max and I can't help but notice the attractive young lady handling the beer sales and the short shorts she's wearing. Colby's group ahead of us is now nowhere in sight. I saw a few of his shots earlier in the round, but I haven't seen them at all since the front nine. I hope the kid is playing well. Joey also sends one of his assistants to the groups behind us to keep them up-to-date with what is going on ahead of them and tells them they are going to have to be patient. There are only two more groups behind us, and the assistant pro tells us they are fine and not in any rush.

I take advantage of the time being taken up by logistics to tell Max about Atlanta.

***

Wendy met us at the airport at 8:00 am. Our flight was departing at 9:15, and she was able to get a ticket after we left her house the night before. We checked in, and although there were still seats available, the flight agent couldn't get the three of us seated together. When we got on the plane, we found someone to swap with so that we could have a row of seats to ourselves.

We were tired, but Wendy took the middle seat and for the entirety of the short flight, she told us everything we could ever want to know about Sammy's parents; why they had adopted her, how they chose her name, where they lived, what their careers were, and multitudes more. By the time I got off the plane, I knew more about Sammy and her parents than I think I would have if we had been married for years. The thing that made me feel the best was that my initial instincts were right on ten years ago. Sammy was everything I had ever imagined and more.

Wendy told us about the time Sammy found out she was adopted. She was twelve and Wendy had just turned thirteen. They were skiing in Colorado, which Sammy's parents had done every year since they were married. Her father had been an avid skier growing up in Vermont, and it was important for him to teach his daughter how to ski. Wendy was the beneficiary of these trips, as well, since they always brought her along. She told us how on this trip, Sammy's parents explained to her that she was adopted. They wanted Wendy there for support since the two of them had been through everything together from the time they were babies. It was their first night of the ski vacation, and they were staying in a nice lodge near the resort. Wendy and Sammy shared the pull-out couch in the living room, while her parents had the bedroom. After dinner, they returned to the condo and told Sammy while sitting around the fireplace. She seemed a little shocked by the news, but didn't say much or show hardly any emotion. Both she and Wendy had no idea. It had been a well-kept secret, and there were so many pictures of Sammy as a baby around the house, she never questioned it. Her parents looked enough like her with similar hair and eye color, so Sammy never imagined they weren't her "real" parents. After Sammy heard everything they had to say, she simply said, "Okay." Then she stood up and started getting ready for bed. Wendy knew that wasn't going to be the end of it, but she figured it was enough for one night and they all went to bed. Wendy could hear Sammy trying to hide her tears when they got in bed.

The next day, they all hit the slopes as usual. Wendy and Sammy always rode the chairlift together, and on their first ride of the day, Sammy talked the entire time. Her parents were behind them on the next chair but couldn't hear anything she was saying. Sammy told Wendy that she didn't ever want to know who her "real" parents were. They obviously didn't want her as a baby, and she didn't want them. Her mom and dad were the best parents in the world and she was so lucky to have them. She felt they would be hurt too much if Sammy ever went to find these other people. Wendy told us it started a change in Sammy. She really grew up after that trip. She seemed to become a more significant young lady, and she had a newfound appreciation for her parents. They became even closer than before, which they hadn't thought possible. Being a pre-teen, Sammy had previously gone through the typical self-imposed separation from them, but since learning of her adoption, she bonded even closer. Wendy loved being around them.

Wendy called Dan and Elizabeth "Liz" Lang on her way to the airport that morning and told them she would be in Atlanta that afternoon and needed to meet with them. Dan was semiretired and worked from home. Liz had a volunteer job she was supposed to be at, but she told Wendy she would reschedule. We all arrived shortly after noon, and Wendy asked us to wait in the rental car until she had a moment to discuss with them in private. She knew they might need a few minutes to gather themselves before we all dropped in on them at once. Wendy stood at the door, rang the bell, and then looked back at us. We could see she was nervous. It was obvious they might not be too excited to meet me, and Wendy hoped she would be able to smooth over the introductions by speaking with them alone first. When they answered the door, they exchanged hugs, but it didn't look like they were overly enthusiastic to have her on their doorstep. She motioned to us in the car and they talked for a few moments, then she waved for us to join her.

We settled in the living room, where the conversation started cool-bordering-on-frigid, but once they heard my side of the story of what had happened a decade ago, they warmed up substantially. I then went into all the details about Cindy and what had brought me to discover who Samantha Lang actually was. I could tell it was all surreal to them. Their only daughter, who died at nineteen ten years ago, had an identical twin sister lying in a hospital in Boston. Admittedly, it sounded like a bad soap opera, but it also struck a nerve. They wanted to return with me later that night to meet her, but I insisted they give me some time to make Cindy aware of this situation. After all, Cindy had just recently learned she lost her mother, who was her only living relative, so laying the rest of this on her might be too much for her to handle. I knew I had to meet with the staff in the psych department to best figure out how to approach her. I wasn't just a doctor on her case, I was emotionally entangled and they would want to discuss how best to approach her with this kind of news. Dan and Liz were being very cooperative, despite how shocking this conversation was. It was almost like they had become immune to shock, and maybe they had after Sammy's car had been found in a Memphis river. Once a parent has lost a child, their lives are never the same, nor should it be. I unfortunately have to see this all too often in the hospital. There's a common numbness to parents who have outlived their children, and the Lang's definitely had that "stare" in their eyes. Recognizing this marker is a talent I have that I hope other people never acquire.

We stayed for over two hours, and when we got ready to leave, Liz hugged me like she had known me my entire life. She was holding back tears, and I had a brief look into what might have been my future if these two strangers could have been significant people in my life. Dan then shook my hand and gave me a hug. He wished me a safe trip home and made me promise I would call them to come to Boston as soon as possible. They said a pleasant good bye to Rob, who barely had anything to say the entire time. It occurred to me that his job was done and he was now just an interested spectator wanting to see how this would all play out. When they said good-bye to Wendy, it was in completely different tones than when they greeted her. I felt the healing between them had accelerated more in the last two hours than it had in the last ten years.

We walked back to the car and Wendy put on her sunglasses. A tear slid down her cheek from beneath her lenses. I put my arm around her as we walked to the car. As soon as we were inside the vehicle with all the doors closed, she broke down entirely.

"I didn't sleep at all last night," she sobbed. "I-I've just been so worried about how this was going to go. But-but I just wasn't ready to feel this way." With that, she began to cry uncontrollably. I squeezed her hand while I drove and Rob rubbed her shoulders from the back seat. It was as though we had known each other our whole lives.

\*\*\*

I am actually getting chocked up on the tee box telling Max this part of the story. I shrug my shoulders, shake my head slightly, and look down the fairway now lined with a larger crowd than I have ever played in front of. I think of Sammy, Cindy, and Wendy as I tee up my ball. I am holding a 3 wood and turn my attention to the shot at hand. It is a slight downhill dogleg left. I chose the 3 wood knowing I can hit a little draw to the corner, and if it catches the fairway, my ball should roll a long way, leaving me a short iron to a large green. I can see the shot in my head better than I have ever done so before. There is a clarity I always knew was available, but my brain has allowed it to get foggy over the years. Today is different, and the confidence I have is almost like a drug. I take my practice swing to get loose, line up, and draw my club back inside my normal driver swing path to make sure I hit the ball from the inside. I generally hit a little draw with this club, and I have to fight from over-swinging. I know I can get a little too quick on the downswing and come over the top, yanking my ball left, so I think, *smooth downswing*, and hit it just as planned. My ball takes off, heading down the right side of the fairway and begins a slow draw to the left. It catches enough of the hill to let it continue on its journey down the fairway. It seems so easy. Why hasn't golf always been like this?

Max still has quite a bit of confidence carrying over from the last bomb he hit on 13, and as he pulls his driver, I know he will be looking to take one over the corner. It is a shot you only hit when you aren't trying to win a tournament, because it is definitely risky. But between the crowd and the adrenaline pumping through his veins, Max doesn't see any other play. He really goes after it again and makes excellent contact, his ball cuts off the corner of the trees and he has plenty of room to clear them. He has a little fade on the ball, and after it flies the corner, it keeps going past the fairway and into the rough, but he has a very short iron left to the green. The crowd has to move out of the way of his ball and they had actually flattened down the rough in the area they'd been standing on, which gives him an even better lie. I realize that if I hadn't been on this incredible role, Max would have been the one to beat today.

Dustin, having nothing to lose, takes a similar line with his driver, but he is able to get the ball to turn right-to-left with a high flight, which puts him directly in the fairway, even closer than Max. The crowd is getting rowdy and lets out a roar as his ball lands. Dustin smiles, and once again we are walking down the fairway like it's the red carpet at the Oscars, complete with people snapping pictures. I am definitely the lead, but my costars are nominated for best supporting actors and have taken the spotlight with their monstrous drives.

*** 

Rob and I got to the airport and walked Wendy to her concourse, which was as far as we could go with her. The bond between us was stronger than steel at this point. We had been through a war of emotions in less than a day, and we knew our lives would forever be linked together. We weren't saying "goodbye" but "see you real soon." She wanted to come to Boston with Dan and Liz as soon as I gave them the OK, and I told her it hopefully wouldn't be too long. We hugged each other and shared a wonderful smile together. There was so much said already, we didn't need to say any more. She then hugged Rob, as well, and thanked him for all his help. He told her it was his pleasure, and he was overjoyed to be a part of this experience. She turned and walked away, and we stood there and watched her head toward the entrance to security. She looked back, waved, and disappeared into the corridor beyond the metal detectors and x-ray machines, then we headed off to the other terminal.

Rob and I had some time to kill before our flights, so we sat at one of the concourse bars, ordered a beer, and sank into our chairs. What a whirlwind the last 24 hours had been. We didn't talk much, and my mind was racing with thoughts of how to gently fill Cindy in on all of this when I got back to the hospital.

Rob's flight back to New York was a little before mine and only a few gates away. I walked him to his plane and couldn't thank him enough for all he had done for me.

"Don't worry about it," he told me. "This has been one of the most rewarding cases I have ever worked on."

"Can I at least pay you for your time and your flights and everything else you put into this?"

He put his hands firmly on my shoulders, looked me in eye, and said simply, "I won't take a penny." Then he smiled and added, "Just promise you'll let me know how your conversation with Cindy goes and keep me updated on everything else, too, okay?"

I smiled gratefully back at him. "I wouldn't dream of keeping you out of the loop."

He nodded and clapped me on the shoulder. "In that case, we're all square and I need to get on the plane before it leaves without me." We both raised a hand in farewell after he got his ticket scanned, then I turned to find my own boarding gate.

It was late that night when I arrived back in Boston, and I decided to go home. I didn't have the strength to go to the hospital, and I knew I would be better at handling everything after getting a good night's rest. Not only that, but since it was my day off, I would also have time to decide how best to bring this all up with Cindy.

***

I walk down the fairway to find my ball had luckily landed just short of a massive divot. I've always agreed with Jack Nicklaus' theory about fairway divots; they should be considered ground-under-repair, and if you land in one, you should be given relief. However, the golf rules don't allow it. Even though I am very close to this divot, it won't impact my shot. There is enough grass between my ball and the leading edge of the divot for me to make a clean shot and get some spin on the ball. I have a pitching wedge in my hand and wish I had a caddy to talk to about the shot. A good caddy can help boost your confidence in certain times during a tournament, and although I've played plenty of golf with caddies, all the college tournaments and the ones I've played in since have been without one. Because you can't exchange any advice with your playing partners, a caddy allows you talk through the shot out loud and helps confirm your thoughts. This is the first time today I feel I want to talk the shot through with someone. I am still playing at the top of my game, and I've made excellent decisions all day, so I do not doubt my ability. Mostly, I am looking to decide between clubs, so I start talking to myself quietly aloud so that nobody else can hear me, but it allows me to get my thoughts straight. "Hit the wedge, choke it down just a little, and take a full shot," I say, and I can feel my confidence rise as I approach my pre-shot routine. I make one of the best-feeling strokes I've made all day, and although I've made thirteen birdies in a row, this shot comes off perfectly. By the time I look up, the ball is going right at the pin. I know it is going to be close. It hits two feet right of the pin and spins left. I think it is going to drop in the hole, but it comes to rest inches from the cup and the crowd surrounding the green lets out a thunderous roar. I feel goose bumps run up and down my arms and neck. God, I love this game!

Max gets to his ball and the crowd has, for the most part, all moved up to the green. He has a good lie in the patted-down rough, and he is able to put another good move on it, but the lack of a tight lie causes him to catch a little flyer and he soars just over the back of the green. He'll have a difficult downhill chip from there, and it'll be hard to stop it once it gets rolling.

Dustin's shot is just a little sand-wedge left to the green. He hits it hard and has a good amount of spin on it. His ball lands a good twenty-five feet over the pin, bounces forward once, but then spins back hard down the hill and somehow manages to stop above the hole. It must have hit an old ball mark or something to keep it from running farther, and it is actually a bad break as now he has a slippery five-footer and I'm sure he would have had a better chance from fifteen feet below the hole. We are all approaching the green from different angles, and I know I need to get back to Max at some point soon to get through the rest of this story. We get to the green, and once again, the crowd is very appreciative of the high level of play they are watching. The applause was becoming a welcome arrival at every green. I begin to wonder how I am going to feel the next time I play golf without it being there, and I know I will really miss it.

Max is next to play, and he hits a good chip, but it picks up speed and I think for sure it will run far off the green. However, as it approaches the pin, we can see it is right on-line and it hits the pin right smack in the center, makes a loud noise, bounces back less than a few inches, and stops. It is one of the best breaks he's had all day. I walk up, pull the pin, and let him putt out a scary-but-smooth par.

Dustin is up, and with only five feet to negotiate for birdie, he has a great chance to make it. He fully expects to make it, anyway, and isn't afraid to give it a good run, so he takes aim and hits it firmly to take any break out of it. As the ball gets closer to the hole, it's ever-so-slightly off-line, and hits the cup with a touch too much speed. If it had been dead center, it might have dropped, but as it catches the right side of the cup, the speed keeps it from going in and it instead lips out and continues downhill a good ten feet. He now has twice as far for par as he did for birdie. Dustin doesn't get as upset as he did earlier in the round. He realizes he doesn't have a prayer of winning—or even finishing in the top ten—so he is just playing for glory at this point and taking it all in stride. He walks down to his ball, marks it, and tries again. This time, he can be more aggressive back uphill, and he is. The ball hits the hole hard, and I think it will lip-out again, but it slams right into the back of the cup and he saves his par.

Mine isn't even a shot worth looking at. I only mark it to get out of my playing partners' way and to be respectful of them knowing once I make it, the crowd would move on to the next hole. I put my ball down, and without even taking a normal stance, I tap it in for another routine birdie. I wish golf had always been this easy!

Hole #15

Par 4 – 424 yards

Max and I finally have a chance to talk again on the way to the 15th tee box, so I go on to tell him what happened next when I got to the hospital early the next morning.

\*\*\*

Bonnie Stewart is the head of the staff psychiatric department at the hospital. She has an MD in psychiatry and loves her job. She's a very attractive woman in her mid-sixty's and a complete workaholic, so I knew she would be in her office when I arrived. It was still my day off, so I was dressed in jeans, sneakers and a golf shirt, not my normal scrubs or white coat.

Bonnie waved me in from her desk. "Good morning, Dr. Peters. What brings you in so early?" She hadn't looked up since I entered her office, and when she did, she peered at me over her glasses. "It must be Miss Smith?"

"Yes," I said. "I have a situation I need to talk to you about, and I really need some advice." I then went on to explain everything to her. It once again took a while to get through this story even though I was getting better at telling it. Bonnie had been with Cindy quite a bit since her awakening, so she was very familiar with everything about her case. However, this was all new information, and I was concerned she was going to tell me to never talk to Cindy about any of it. I knew that wasn't going to happen, but the unfounded fear of it was still rooted deeply in my mind. We have a hospital policy to not get personally involved with patients, and I knew she was going to have some strong recommendations on how I approached Cindy.

When I was finished, she took off her glasses, looked me straight in the eye, and told me she released Cindy from the ICU yesterday to a private room on one of the lower floors. She said she no longer considered her "suicidal," and since she was recovering fine, there wasn't a need to have her on twenty-four-hour watch. Cindy had never been suicidal—depressed, yes, but that was to be expected—still the hospital didn't want to take any chances with a woman they knew so little about. The time Bonnie and Cindy spent together the day before had been very productive. Cindy needed some good therapy, and except for her first few hours after waking, there had never been an issue with her mentally. Long story short, Bonnie felt strongly she would be able to handle all this new information immediately. She thought it would even help the healing process, knowing there was someone out there she could consider "family," no matter how distant they actually were.

She came around from behind her desk, put her hand on mine, and said, "Jim, she's a very intelligent woman who's been dealt a lousy hand. You're a great doctor and you have a way about you that makes people feel comfortable. I wish we could get you to teach bedside manner classes, so I'm not at all worried about you letting her know everything you've told me. I am a little concerned about you, though. This is obviously something you've been suppressing for ten years, and I don't know that you've ever gotten over her twin sister."

She was right, but I said, "Yeah, it's been a big part of my life. And you probably understand that since it was only within the last 48 hours I learned what happened to Samantha, I've had a ton of emotions come back to the surface." I took a deep breath. "But I really think that helping Cindy through this will help me, too."

Bonnie smiled. "That's what I was hoping to hear." She patted my hand and sat back down behind her desk. "I think you're absolutely right. Telling Cindy everything you have told me might be the best therapy for both of you. But remember, if you ever need to talk things out in the future, my door is always open."

I thanked her with all sincerity, then left to go find Cindy.

I was relieved and ecstatic with the way this conversation had turned out, but now I had to focus on the next one I was about to have. I decided today was as good a day as any to jump into it. I was able to tell Bonnie all of this in less than thirty minutes, but I felt it could take most of the day to get it all out to Cindy. The thought of telling her was making me nervous, though. I'd been playing out parts of this conversation in my head beginning on the plane last night, but there was so much uncertainty on how it would be taken that I knew it would just have to play out as it happened.

I stepped onto the second floor—where Cindy's new room was—and took a moment to calm myself down. I was very familiar with the staff on this floor due to the fact this is where most my patients come post-op, unless they have more serious problems. I'd even dated more than a few of the nurses on this floor. One such nurse was Monica, and there she was as I came off the elevator. A very warm and welcoming smile bloomed on her face when she saw me.

"Hello, stranger," she said playfully, and I knew immediately that I was going to have to sidestep any conversation concerning why I hadn't called in such a long time. I didn't really have much fun the one time I took Monica out, and the older I get, the less time I tend to waste with women I have nothing in common with; so I simply didn't have time to waste making small talk with her.

I exchanged pleasantries and quickly asked her what room Cynthia Smith was in before she could engage in the conversation I knew was foremost in her mine. "Oh, is she one of your patients?" she asked.

"Yes, I helped with her surgery the day she arrived here. What room is she in?" I tried to keep it as professional as possible.

She smiled and gestured vaguely down the hall. "She's in room 208."

"Thanks," I said, and without further ado, I was off to find Cindy.

I got to Cindy's room and was greeted with the warm smile I'd been missing most, followed by her quick banter, "I thought maybe you forgot about me."

"I'm sorry I haven't been around, I had a family issue come up a couple days ago. How are you doing?" I didn't want to blurt out that it was really *her* family issue, not mine.

"Much better," she told me. "I'm feeling like I'm actually getting out of here someday. They tell me most of my injuries are healing fine, except my right leg, and with some therapy and crutches, I could be released in less than a week." She was smiling with that thought, and I tried to imagine what her life must have been like since she came out of the coma. I realized I had no idea of the amount of emotions she'd been through.

"I finally got in touch with my supervisor where I was supposed to show up for work last month, they wondered where I've been. Luckily they told me I had a job as soon as I was ready, even though they went ahead and filled my position a few weeks ago" she told me. It was a large company, and they could make room for her anytime, which gave her the assurance that she needed. She also told me she'd been in touch with one of her friends back in California and her family attorney, so she felt like she was slowly putting her life back together. The loss of her mother was still very much on her mind, and I could see Cindy get upset when she thought of her, but overall, I was impressed with how well she was dealing with everything.

Her hair had almost grown in completely, covering her scar, and more than once she made comments on how much she was looking forward to getting it styled again, as well as having a manicure and pedicure and spending a day at the spa.

"What, you don't like our 'spa' here?" I asked with mock indignation. She laughed. I smiled congenially, and then sighed. She was as ready for this conversation as she would ever be, so I sat down on the end of bed and braced myself to give her the news. "Cindy, I have some things I need to tell you."

She suddenly turned very serious and said, "I know." This took me by surprise, to say the least. Cindy continued, "I asked the nurses in the ICU a lot of questions about you, since you visited so often, and I heard them talking. I know I remind you of someone, and it appears that while I was in that coma, you thought maybe I was someone close to you. Is that right?"

"Well, yes, that's part of it. Nurses can be very talkative, can't they?" I grinned slightly.

Cindy, however, wasn't smiling at all. "Was it an old girlfriend?"

"Kind of," I said. I hadn't imagined she had any idea, but this made it easier to lead into the story I needed to tell her, and I knew she could have no idea what was coming next. "How would you like to go for a walk? Or, more accurately," I corrected myself, glancing at her casted right leg, "a wheelchair ride outside?"

Her whole face lit up at the suggestion. "I'd love to!"

"Let me arrange it with the staff real quick and we can go out on the grounds to get some fresh air." I was back and putting her in her wheelchair in less than a minute. I handed her the robe at the end of her bed and the slippers from the closet. I realized she didn't have anything here at all. I had forgotten that except for a few items from her wallet, everything had been destroyed in the accident. The police had told her the guy in the other car had been distracted on his cell phone and lost control of his car, which caused the accident. The DA was pursuing vehicular manslaughter chargers, but still hadn't filed anything yet. They promised to keep her posted. As I pushed her down the hall, she told me her attorney had informed her that there was a substantial amount of money left to her from her parents, as well as a life insurance policy naming her the beneficiary. I knew the money would help, but she didn't want it. There wasn't enough money in the world to replace her mother and best friend. She again became quiet.

I searched for a change of subject and settled on the weather. "Look how sunny it is out there." I nodded toward a window. "It'll be nice and warm for our little stroll." She smiled over her shoulder at me.

When we got outside, Cindy put her arms out to embrace the air. Being in a hospital can make you forget how nice nature can look, smell, and feel. As she turned her face skyward and beamed at the open air, with nothing but child-like bliss. I could only imagine how much she was enjoying leaving the hospital for the first time in over a month. I walked her over to a nice spot on the grounds with a lovely wooden bench and stopped.

"Is it alright if I sit on the bench instead of in this chair?" Cindy asked.

"I don't see why not," I answered, then helped her from the wheelchair. She was becoming quite good at using her one good leg, so she didn't need much assistance. When I had her settled, I pushed the wheelchair out of the way and took a seat next to her. For a minute or two, we both sat there and admired the huge oaks lining the hospital. All their leaves shimmered lightly in a subtle breeze, and they provided the perfect amount of shade.

"This is wonderful," she finally said, breaking the silence.

"I'm glad you're enjoying it," I answered, still not yet looking at her. Another minute of silence followed, which I eventually brought myself to end. "Cindy, this something I have to tell you about"

She cut me off, "about that old girlfriend I reminded you of?"

"And about you."

I began with the golf tournament in Memphis over ten years ago and the run-in with a beautiful girl named Samantha. I didn't leave anything out, except how much they looked alike. That would come later. I talked for a while and occasionally asked how she was doing. She assured me that she was fine, but each time seemed impatient that I'd stopped my narration just to ask about her wellbeing. When I got to the part of the story where she entered the hospital, I could tell she was putting it together.

"You thought I was Samantha." She didn't have to ask, she simply stated this as fact.

"Yes," I said, "but it wasn't until the day they took off your bandages that I was convinced you were her, and only after you awoke did I realize you weren't." I went through all the details about Rob searching for information on her, how just in the last few days we had discovered her mother in Montreal. She knew her birth mother was from Canada, and she knew she had died during her delivery, so none of this was too shocking. But when I told her there were two daughters born that day and that she was one half of a set of identical twins, it hit her like a ton of bricks.

"Samantha? She was my sister?" I nodded sadly, unable to form any words, and she began to cry. "Are you sure? How the hell could that happen?" She was truly upset, and I was afraid it might have been too soon to tell her. Neither of us had any tissues, and I looked in vain for something to offer her. In the end, she used the sleeve of her robe to wipe her eyes and nose, and I promised to get her a new one. She laughed a little and said, "I feel like a three-year-old, wiping my nose on my sleeve." I tried to offer an apology for not being better prepared, but she waved it away. "There'll be plenty of time to get a new robe—or wash this one. Please, tell me the rest." Her strength constantly amazed me.

I continued all the way through to meeting Dan, Liz, and Wendy. I told her about everything, and especially how they wanted to come to Boston to meet her. She was shocked. "*This* was the family issue you had to leave town for two days ago?"

"Yeah, I guess it was more your family issue, but I couldn't just tell you that without the rest of the details." I pulled out my phone and showed her the two pictures I've kept in there of Sammy. Perhaps I should have let go of them long ago but now I was glad I had them. She stared at them with amazement and I watched the tears return to her eyes.

She grinned appreciatively and shook her head. "No, I suppose you couldn't have." She continued to look at the pictures with amazement, "I used to have that same haircut, that's really weird. Can you please forward these to me so I'll have them?"

"Of course" I told her.

***

The 15$^{th}$ hole is a blur. Because this part of the story is so intense, Max and I have stayed very close to each other so I could tell him everything about that conversation. We all hit our driver's off the tee. Dustin and I were in the fairway, Max just into the short rough, and we all hit the green. The two of them make easy pars without threatening a birdie, and I sink a 15-footer to keep the streak alive. Except for the loud rounds of applause, it might well have been just Max and me out enjoying a Sunday morning stroll through another golf course. But today isn't anything like a typical round of golf. I am 15 under par through 15 holes, and the reality of shooting 54 is trying hard to take over my brain. I won't let it. The idea of getting to the end of this story with Max is too important, and it's the perfect way to suppress those "54" thoughts.

We continued toward the next tee with me telling Max how Cindy and I spent the better part of the day talking.

***

She had hundreds of questions. At one point, we went to the cafeteria for lunch, and then I accompanied her to an hour of physical therapy, but we never stopped talking. She wanted to know everything, and she made me call Dan and Liz. I told them I was there with Cindy and she wanted to talk to them. They both got on the other end of the line, and I gave the phone to Cindy. I started to walk away to give her some privacy, but she grabbed my arm and

122

mouthed the words, "Please stay," so I sat back down. She started off introducing herself, but within seconds she was crying, and I was sure they were, too. The conversation was very short. She nodded a lot, and I knew they could tell she physically couldn't talk, apparently, they were dealing with the same range of emotions. She gathered herself and said, "Okay," and then hung up the phone. I imagined they said they would talk later after they had a chance to calm down a bit. Cindy began to cry uncontrollably, and I did the first thing I could think of; I held her tight. A warm, human body was what she needed most right now, and honestly, I needed it too. We were silent for a long time, just sitting there with her in my arms. She finally sat up and wiped my shirt—which was covered in tears—with her clean sleeve.

"Sorry," she choked out.

"Don't be," I said. "You've been through a lot today."

"And I'm going to go through more." I gave her a confused look and she clarified.

"They're coming up tonight, Wendy too."

***

# Hole #16

## Par 4 – 366 yards

Max is so enthralled by this story, he apparently can't even fathom golf. I am trying to get ready for my next shot on the 16th tee, but I can see in his face he doesn't want me to stop talking. However, I do just long enough to think about the next shot, which is another straight-ahead, rather short par 4. It's not really reachable today playing just about 375 yards to the pin, but a big drive will leave a great opportunity to get up and down for birdie. Even a shot off-line won't create many problems, as the trees are farther off the fairway and it's very wide open. I rip a driver as hard as I can. It goes well over 300 yards, since it's playing downwind and I manage to catch it with enough of the face of the club to keep it straight. Dustin and Max follow my lead and both bomb their drives in the direction of the green. We are all in good shape.

I look up to see that we now have at least a couple dozen golf carts following the progress of our group. They stay far ahead, and people are hanging on the backs of them to get to their next vantage point. It is quite the scene. The beer cart even has to go back and restock, and I imagine the sales are really good for the course at this point in time. Joey seems very happy things are still in control, and I am sure he has his hands full.

As we walk up the fairway, Dustin is closer to us than he has been all day, and I don't see the need to stop talking with him there. I figure it can't hurt to have him along, and I'm sure he will be lost with this conversation, anyway. He is a bit too late to the meeting to interject anything, but all the same, he seems glad to be there. I am trying to wrap up the meat of this story, so I tell Max about Dan and Liz's visit to the hospital.

\*\*\*

They came to visit that night, and arrived at the hospital by 9:00 pm. As soon as Cindy had told me they were coming, I had arranged for a late visit with the chief of staff. Normally on this floor, visitors were limited to the hours between 8:00 am and 8:00 pm; but since I asked—and since Cindy had a private room—he was fine with it. After that, I went to doctor's locker room to clean up, and then I ordered some food for Cindy and me from a restaurant around the corner, thinking she could use a good meal that didn't consist of hospital food. We finished dinner about the same time Dan and Liz arrived. I greeted them with a hug and introduced them to Cindy, then I left the room to give them some time to get acquainted. I could hear their sobs as I shut the door on my way to wait by the nurses' station. I made nervous small talk with the nurse on duty, Marc, for nearly an hour. He'd worked there for a few years, and we had played together once in a hospital golf tournament I had been talked into running. It turned out to be a lot of fun, but Marc was a lousy golfer.

Finally, I looked up and saw Wendy coming down the hall. She smiled and gave me a small wave. I couldn't believe it was just the day before when we had last seen each other. I didn't imagine I would see her so soon. She came up and hugged me. I took her to Cindy's room and knocked on the door. Dan opened it and gave Wendy a huge hug, then he held her hand, walked her to Cindy's bed, and introduced her as her cousin Wendy. The emotion in the room was palpable. I turned to walk out and give them more family bonding time, but Dan put his hand on my shoulder and asked me to stay. I hesitated. I truly wanted to witness this experience, but I was afraid to get any more emotionally involved. Then, I glanced at the faces around me and realized that I was already too far in to try to keep from being involved now. Slightly apprehensive of the amount of tissues I knew I was about to go through with this family, I nodded and agreed to stay.

What followed was an uncontrollable outpouring of sentiment unlike anything I had ever seen. There was a small undercurrent of sadness from all parties, but trumping this was pure, unadulterated joy. Once they all calmed down enough that they could hold a conversation, they couldn't stop talking. There wasn't any real blood relation between any of them and Cindy, but it didn't matter. She was the identical twin to Dan and Liz's daughter and Wendy's cousin and best friend; and the Lang's were a new support Cindy could use to help the healing process. It was evident after only a few short minutes that they were family, and nobody would ever be able to convince them otherwise.

***

Max is starting to get emotional on me, and Dustin is simply confused. I know he wants to know who these people I'm talking about are, and why Max is so choked up over them. But this isn't the time to backtrack, so I'll let Dustin draw his own conclusions. He walks off toward his ball as Max and I go to ours. I tell Max how the Lang's stayed in Boston for a week and spent all their time at the hospital until Cindy was released.

***

They made arrangements to help Cindy get an apartment, and they moved her into it before they went back to Atlanta. Wendy stayed only two days before having to return to her family, but she promised to come back soon.

Cindy had healed well enough and had done plenty of physical therapy that the hospital felt she was ready to move on. I spent very little time away from her for the rest of her stay in the hospital, and I, too, helped move her into the new apartment. She was able to get around on crutches, and within a week or two, she could be off them completely. Cindy was getting used to her new arrangements, but she wanted to start working as soon as she could. It would be

126

good for her to start her new life, and work was a critical factor in doing just that.

***

We once again have golf shots to deal with, and although it seems like the story of Cindy is the priority, we know it is actually a means of making it through the golf course, so we focus as needed. Dustin is next to play, and he flies his ball past the green. He has too much adrenaline, I figure, as the crowd is now too big to count. I take it as a sign to check my tempo and not let my elevated heart rate allow me to lose control of my swing.

I am up next, and it is like I am throwing darts. I check my yardage and I'm be damned if my radar gun doesn't say I have exactly "54" yards to the pin! This number is coming at me like a ton of bricks and it's all I can do to remove it from my mind and try to concentrate on the shot and not the number! I throw a lob wedge high above the green and watch my ball come down softly to sit near the pin. The crowd once again shows its enthusiasm, and all I can do is smile and I tip my hat, to which Max tips his back at me. He then takes aim at the flag and hits a good shot, but he has a bit more on the shot than needed, too, and his ball lands just on the back of the green. It takes one jump toward the rough, but catches what appears to be the last strand of grass on the first cut, which gives it just enough to spin it back onto the green. Still, he will have a lengthy birdie putt.

We gradually surround the green. Max and I mark our balls and get out of the way for Dustin to make his approach chip, which he does without too much trouble. I realize the kid has a damn good short game as he nestles his ball three feet from the hole. As he walks up to his ball, he looks at me and says, "How about I just putt out?"

"Go for it," I tell him, knowing he is smart enough to get out of the way

127

and doesn't want to follow me.  It is the courteous thing to do, and it wouldn't have been an option had he been in contention, so I give him respect for requesting it.  He marks his ball, wipes it clean with his towel, replaces it, and rams it home for a par.

I smile at him.  "Good job."

Max's putt runs by the hole a good five feet, and he, too, putts out, even though I am now farthest away and technically my turn, he's allowed to putt out and it's the right thing to do in this situation.  He also makes par, and now I am there, trying to make another birdie.  I have about eight feet left with a slight right-to-left break.  I walk around it from both sides, set it up, and hit it well.  By the time I look up, my ball is about three feet from the cup and isn't breaking as much as my comfort-level would have liked.  I stare with anticipation as it seems to take forever covering those last few feet.  With only a couple of inches to go, I start to think it isn't going to drop.  Then, it miraculously catches the right-hand lip of the cup and starts to turn left around the back of the hole.  Everyone gasps as we all think it would stay out, but at the very last turn, the ball drops into the cup with a happy little *kerplunk*!

Max walks the pin back to the hole as I took my ball out.  He gives me a high-five and says, "You're making it really interesting out here!"

Hole #17

Par 3 – 199 yards


Everyone is hurrying up to the 17th green, which isn't very far from the 16th green. The three of us walk the farther distance to the tee box. This one is a difficult par 3, with just under 200 yards to a small green surrounded by extensive bunkers. The shot requires distance and precision to make birdie. This is a hole you can easily make a bogey on and still have hit a good shot. Many tournaments have been lost on this hole alone. I know it and remove that thought as quickly as it enters my mind. As the crowd gets settled by the green, I take a moment to tell Max how the next few weeks passed with Cindy.


\*\*\*


We stayed in close contact. There wasn't any romance between us, but as she was getting better, the thought became more and more prevalent in my mind. I was undeniably attracted to her, but I didn't want to push the issue. As much as she loved being around me, I could tell she was afraid of letting me in too close. For my part, my emotions were all confused. I didn't know if we were supposed to be together or if we were supposed to be like siblings.

The Lang's and Wendy had been back on two different occasions. Cindy was going to go visit each of them soon, but she was just starting to get around without her crutches and was now working almost full-time. We would talk to each other daily, although I hadn't seen her for a week by the time this tournament started.


\*\*\*


"She thinks Dan and Liz might come up this weekend, and Wendy was

129

talking about it, too," I tell Max.

"Wait, that's it?" Max looks slightly confused at the abrupt end to the story.

"For now, yeah."

"Oh wow. I was expecting something different today but this is truly an incredible story." He claps me on the shoulder and says, "She seems literally like the girl of your dreams!"

I ponder that thought and just smile back at my friend.

Joey has everyone settled in now, so he waves us up. I take out a four iron and start getting focused. I've hit five here a lot, but today the wind is coming from our left and a little in our face. I figure I can hit the four choked down with a slightly open face to knock it a little higher and allow it to sit softly on the green. That's the way I see it, and sure enough, when I look up it is on its way to the pin like a GPS-locked missile. I think for sure it'll be good, and I figure I will have another great opportunity once this ball settles in. The crowd is already clapping and yelling, the noise level is rising steadily, and I am still holding my follow-through. The ball comes down with authority right at the pin. It strikes the flag with full force, enough so that we can hear it back on the tee, and the flag shakes violently back and forth. My ball jumps hard to the left and rolls all the way to the side of the green before stopping up against the collar.

I groan. This is an incredibly bad break. If it had missed the pin, it probably would have ended up no more than a few feet away; but now I have a good 30-plus foot putt to go.

Max immediately interjects, "Don't worry about it Jim, you can make that putt in your sleep."

"Yeah, that'll be fine." I am surprisingly not upset. I have had great luck today, and I know I will have a chance at this. I've had that putt before, and I know the break very well.

Max smiles at me, noting the sincerity in my voice. "That's the spirit!"

I smile back at him and move off the tee, starting to put the club back in my bag. Although not upset about the shot, my adrenaline has developed a mind of its own and is now coursing full-force through my veins. I try to relax, but my heart is beating fast.

Max takes the tee. He seems more upset about my shot than I am, but he gets it together and hits a high draw against the wind with a five iron. He plays it well, but when his ball hits the green, it doesn't check but instead rolls toward the back of the green. He is outside my ball and has a different angle, so I won't be able to go to school on him, but I can at least get a good read on the speed of the green from there.

Dustin hits last, and he also hits a five iron. He is younger and stronger, no doubt about it. His five iron flies right at the pin, but keeps going and lands in the bunker over the green. We walk up to the green in complete silence. I think the spectators are afraid of what happened to my shot and they don't want to upset me. Funny, but I'm not thinking about it at all. Instead, I am contemplating what Max said to me about Cindy, and he's right. She *is* everything I ever wanted in a woman. If I hadn't met Sammy before Cindy, I wouldn't have stopped at anything to be with her. I've been letting Sammy keep me from Cindy, and what I've failed to realize is perhaps Sammy's role in my life was to get me to Cindy. Perhaps this is a bit narcissistic but now it seems logical.

I nod to myself, settling my internal debate. The next time I see Cindy, I'm not going to tap-dance around my emotions any longer. I'm going to tell her exactly how I feel, and to hell with the consequences.

My confidence soars at this prospect. I'm walking with renewed hope, like I have just birdied the first hole and have all the anticipation of that infamous 54. As I get to the green, the applause is now as loud as I've heard all day. People are yelling all sorts of encouragement.

"You can do it, Jim!"

"It's all yours, Doc!"

"Show 'em how it's done, bud!"

I scan the crowd and can't believe how many of the other players who have finished ahead of me are now there, cheering me on. I *am* going to make this putt. Then I'm going to birdie 18, celebrate like there's no tomorrow, and find my girl!

Even though Dustin is closest to the pin, being in the bunker we motion to him to play onto the green and he is happy to do so. He once again puts his short game skills to the test and flies his ball from the bunker with perfect precision. It stops less than a foot away. He runs up to the green, pulls the flag and drops it to the ground away from the line of either of the other two putts, with only his right hand on the club he puts his sand wedge up against his ball and taps it in with the leading edge. The crowd likes this kid, and both Max and I applaud along with the rest of them. He picks up the flag and tips his hat.

"Do you want me to tend the pin for either of you?" he asks.

"I'm good," says Max.

"Me, too."

Dustin takes the pin with him to the edge of the green, well out of the way of both of our putts.

Max is slightly away, and he is already over his ball. He has taken a good look at it and doesn't want to waste any time. He strokes it well and gets it going on-line with a touch too much speed and not enough break. His ball travels about 8 feet too far, and once again, he has a difficult comeback putt. He again elects to finish out, which is his way of telling me he knows I'll make mine. He negotiates the eight feet with ease, and I am now faced with the longest putt for birdie I've seen all day.

All I can think about is Cindy. I keep imagining seeing her again, and as I look over the challenge at hand, I again have a spike in confidence. I make

132

sure to breathe deeply, take one more look at the hole, and then send the little white ball on its way. The putt takes forever to get there, but it is right on-line, the speed looks great, and I don't move until it looks like it is going to drop in. I start to raise my putter in victory, knowing it's going to drop. Then, with an inch to go, my ball suddenly runs out of speed and stops less than half a rotation away from falling in the cup.

I freeze with my putter only halfway to being over my head. This one isn't going to fall in like the others did. The crowd sighs, and I stand there, stunned. Finally, I shake myself from my reverie and begin a slow walk toward my ball. There is a small smattering of applause, but apparently nearly everyone is in shock. As I get to the ball, I glare at it with a grimace on my face, like it's the balls fault it didn't have enough momentum to get to the hole. I place my putter up against it, take my normal stance, and then do something I've done a hundred times before. I take my right leg and throw it over the putter shaft so the putter is now sticking between my legs with my back to the hole, and I putt the ball backwards, between my legs into the cup. It is a cocky move, but with my birdie run over, and it is my way of saying that this has been incredibly fun and the crowd cheers uncontrollably.

I walk off the green and say to Max, "Well, maybe I can eagle 18 to shoot 54."

He gives me a strange look at these words. "Jim, birdie gets you a 54."

"What?"

"Remember? This is a par 71. You don't have to birdie every hole to get a 54, you just have to birdie one more!"

I had completely spaced that! I was thinking I had to birdie them all to shoot 54, but he's right. I only need one more birdie, and there's a reachable par five coming up.

"You can do it, Jim!" I hear someone yell again, then another person interjects, "Come on, Peters, it's yours for the taking!" Everyone starts rushing ahead to get up the fairway.  And they're right; I can make one more birdie.

## Hole #18

### Par 5 – 578 yards

We walk up to the 18th tee box and put our bags down. I grab my driver as Dustin walks up to me with his hand held out. I shake it and he very sincerely says, "Jim, in case I don't get to tell you later, it's been a real pleasure playing with and watching you today. Thank you for allowing me to be a part of it."

All I can think of to say to such a compliment is, "Thank you." I inject as much gratitude into that phrase as is possible, and the smile I receive in return shows he understands how deeply I mean it. He then shakes hands with Max and thanks him, as well.

Max turns to me, reaches out his hand, grins at me, and says, "Let's finish strong" which is something we've said so often to each other on numerous 18th tee boxes over the years.

I nod in agreement, tee up my ball, look at my playing partners, and say, "Hit 'em great, boys."

I think about playing it safe and hitting a three wood off the tee, but then quickly dismiss the idea. I've been hitting my driver incredibly well all day, and I owe it to myself to stick with it. I need one more birdie to shoot that infamous 54, I know it, everyone knows it. Give the thought just enough to move on and get into the hole, a good par 5, but it can be reached in two with a long, straight tee shot. There is a bunker protecting the green from the front left, which does come into play on the second shot if I have a chance to go for it, but the shot at hand is getting a driver in the fairway. I've worked hard on my pre-shot routine over the years, and never has having trust in it been more important than right now. My mind is crystal clear. I stand behind the ball, pick my line, and start in on the shot. I set my club, take one waggle, put the club behind the ball, draw the club back, swing down and through the ball, and watch it spring off my club. It seems like I am in slow motion, which I really like. It makes me feel like I'm connected with every movement and staying firmly in the moment. My ball takes off straight down the fairway, and I know I've caught it well. Most of the crowd has moved down the fairway and out of the way with a bit of stubborn shepherding on Joey's part. They begin clapping, and I love that sound. I watch the ball land in the fairway, and its long. My heart is beating harder than it has all day, but I am very in control of my emotions and keeping them in check. I'm almost home. I feel like Tiger Woods must have felt at the 1997 Masters when he dominated the field and won by 12 strokes. Afterwards, he was quoted as saying how important it was to finish strong, and he was internally screaming at himself to stay in the game, finish the round. I feel similar now, and although I am enjoying this moment, I keep saying to myself; *It isn't over. It isn't over!*

I step away from the tee box and let Max take his position. He just smiles at me and gives the "nice shot" look I've seen a thousand times. Max is holding a three wood. He is playing great, and although it isn't possible for him to beat me today, he knows he has a good chance at finishing second and he was protecting that possibility. Max can probably lock up second with just a par, so hitting the three wood is a smart play. He hits a nice draw up the right side of the fairway, and it moves back toward the center, his ball ending up about thirty yards short of mine but on a similar line. He is in perfect position to lay-up on his next shot, which will set him up for an easy wedge to the green.

Dustin takes his place. He has his driver in-hand and has nothing to lose by going for it. He is solidly out of contention and just wants to finish strong. He goes after it and pulls his ball a little up the left side of the fairway, but it goes a long way. His ball lands just in the first cut of rough, and he'll have a good angle to the green. He actually outdrove me, but my angle is closer to the green.

Max and I have our bags on our shoulders, and instead of taking off ahead of Dustin like we've been doing all day, we wait for him to grab his bag and walk up the fairway with us. We have bonded through this round, and it is important for us to finish together. Dustin is thankful and smiles as we wait for him to join us. Nothing has to be said; this is a glorious day, we are three hunters returning from the kill, and we just have to bring it on home. Everyone is scurrying up ahead of us to get to the green and watch the finish. We all enjoy this moment; it's what every golfer plays for.

Max turns to me and asks, "Is she here?"

"I don't think so," I tell him.

Dustin looks at us and simply says, "Who?"

"Jim's mystery girl," Max responds, not trying to hide the conversation like we have been most of the day. "He's been telling me a story for eighteen holes now about the girl of his dreams, and I mean that in the most literal sense."

Dustin looks surprised and asks, "Is that what you two have been talking about all day?" He seems shocked. Apparently, it never occurred to him to spend a tournament of this stature talking about a girl. Max and I look at each other, then Max winks at me and turns toward Dustin, puckers his lips, and makes a smacking sound like he is blowing Dustin a kiss.

Dustin looks slightly offended, so I jump in and say, "He means KISS. K-I-S-S, Keep It Simple Stupid." I glance, half reproving, half amused, at Max. "Girls keep it real for us. It's better than discussing golf all day. We're playing golf, so the best conversation is focused on something we really *like* to talk about." Dustin seems taken aback by our simplistic way of getting around the golf course, but in reality, it isn't simple at all. It is something we have worked for years to perfect. Even when I play alone, I keep my mind on things outside of golf, and it makes the game more enjoyable. Only late at night when I crawl into bed do I allow myself the pleasure of playing the game over in my head. I guess it is my take on counting sheep. I am always asleep by the end of the round.

"Besides," I continue, "it seems that little lady in white has been keeping a close eye on you, anyway."

"Who?" Dustin asks.

"The girl hanging with your parents."

Dustin looks toward the green, finds his parents, and says, "There's nobody with them."

I looked up, and I can see his parents off to the left-hand side of the green. It takes me a minute to find the girl in white, and in fact, she is clear across on the other side of the green. "Oh, I thought she was your girlfriend. She was standing with your parents earlier."

He looks at me like I'm crazy. "I wish" he says. "I don't have a girlfriend. They usually think I'm too intense and don't stick around very long." Max laughs. Dustin looks annoyed again and says, "Do you think that's funny?"

"No, no!" Max sputters out between his giggles. He looks at me and says, "You're talking about the girl in the white dress, right?" I nod and he states, "That's Vanessa."

"WHAT?!" I shout at him.

Dustin's face turns back and forth between the two of us and Max explains, "The girl in the white dress is Vanessa. She's been keeping her distance, trying not to distract us. I had planned on telling you about her throughout the entire round, but it was obvious Cindy was the bigger story. After all, it's been ten years in the making."

I am shocked. It explains Max's newfound calmness on the golf course, and I realize he has been playing for a crowd of one the whole game. I don't think I've ever met a girl he's dated at a golf course, since he never mixed the two except for in the conversations we've had.

We are now in the middle of the fairway next to Max's ball. He puts his bag on the ground, grabs a five iron, and is going to lay it up to a good wedge distance. He is standing over his ball, wagging his club back and forth, when he looks me dead in the eye and says, "We got engaged last week." My jaw drops open, and I try unsuccessfully to formulate a coherent response. Max looks down at his ball, draws his club back, and whacks it perfectly down the fairway. He smirks and says, "Don't be so shocked. I'm allowed." He grabs his bag and starts walking away. Dustin, too, takes off toward his ball, but it takes me a moment to start walking. Max looks back at me and smiles. "Come on, old man, you've got a few more shots to play."

Max is engaged. Max is engaged! That thought continues playing over and over in my head like a broken record. He stops in front of me, just to the right of my ball, and waits for me to get there. Dustin is setting up for his shot, and all I can do is stare at Max and grin. I look up to the green and can see Vanessa standing there behind the green. Her hat is in her hands now, and although I can't really see her very well from where we are, I can easily see her striking hair glowing a reddish copper in the sunlight.

"Fuckin' congratulations," is all I can say. He knows I mean it like, "Why the hell didn't you tell me sooner?!" and, "Oh my God!" all mixed into one. It takes supreme force of will to get ready for my next shot. I don't even see Dustin hit, but I hear his shot and as I turn around to see it, the sound tells me that he hit a three wood, which means he is going for the green. I look up toward the green and I see his ball land hard in the bunker. He hit a great shot, but needed to play it a little farther right. Still, he's in good position.

I reach into my bag and grab my three wood. There isn't any other play. I am far too close to not go for it. The only trouble is the bunker, and although I haven't been in one all day, I am very confident I can clear it; and if not, my sand game is good. I am about to start my routine. Max and I are alone in the middle of the fairway, Dustin is off to the side, and a large crowd of well over a hundred people are surrounding the green. My heart is beating with a little more intensity, and although I'm sure Max's news will help, the excitement of the day is coming to a climax.

I look at Max again, and as I turn back to my ball, Max says, "I'm not asking, but I fully expect you to be my best man."

I stop and don't move for a moment, then take my grip on my club, look at Max, and say, "Since you're not asking, I'm not answering. Just tell me where and when." I then step up to my ball, look at the green, back at my ball, and hit it as hard as I can. It takes off on a great line, starting just inside the right side of the bunker, ever-so-slightly fades to the right, and I have the thought that I will have an eagle putt. It's amazing how much can go through your head in a split second. As my ball flies through the air, I think of making the putt for a 53. I've never considered shooting a 53. Yes, the thought of 54 is always the dominant thought when shooting that "perfect" round, but 53 had never been a conscious thought until this very second. However, it easily disappears as I see my ball just barely clear the top of the bunker on the right side, it hits the upslope between the sand and the green, and shoots straight up in the air. From my vantage point, I think for sure it will bounce forward on the green, but it jumps straight up and comes down almost exactly where it hit, and with one more small bounce, it rolls back into the bunker. The crowd goes from a loud cheer to a loud sigh. I don't let it bother me. I turn to Max, we share an easy smile, and I am so happy for him that being in the bunker doesn't even make a dent in my attitude.

We once again throw our bags on our shoulders and walk toward Max's ball. It is amazingly quiet. We don't speak at all. Dustin is walking up ahead of us in the direction of the green. My heartbeat is gaining in intensity. The day is perfect, and the scene is better than anything I could have imagined. I take it all in. I can see my ball in the corner of the bunker and Dustin's resting in the middle of it. Max breaks away from me and approaches his third shot. He has about 120 yards from a great lie in the fairway. He hits a smooth pitching wedge just left of the flag, it comes to rest no more than twelve feet from the hole. The crowd claps with great enthusiasm.

Dustin stops and watches the shot. I wait for Max to catch up to me and we walk to the green together. The crowd starts clapping slowly as we get within fifty yards of the green, and then they let it all out as we reach the front of the green. Max puts his bag on the side of the green while Dustin and I approach the bunker. Dustin is first to play. He takes a little extra time, and I realize the number of people watching is a new situation for all of us. I can tell by the strained look on his face that he must be experiencing the same pounding in his chest that I am. It's a strange feeling; half not wanting to screw up in front of so many people, half ecstatic at the thought of impressing so many people.

Dustin settles down over the shot and makes his swing. He catches just a bit too much sand, and although his ball makes the green, he hit a little too fat to leave him a good run at birdie. He gets out of the bunker and rakes his footprints and swing divot. I wait until he finishes and tosses the rake to my side of the bunker. I look over the shot in preparation. I step into the bunker, feeling my feet sink into the sand, and look at the pin. I am digging my feet into the sand when I see nothing but white directly in line with the pin, so I look up and catch my first real glimpse of Vanessa. She is five feet off the green, and I look at her face. She really is beautiful. Her long red hair is shining in the sun, and I can't help but notice what an incredible body she has. I smile at her, and her face lights up as she smiles back. I try my best to congratulate her via eye contact, and I think she understands.

I turn my focus back to the ball. I have a good lie and feel confident about the shot. I look at the pin, consciously *don't* look at Vanessa, and then look again at my ball. My breathing is right on track, despite my heart pounding like crazy, and I swing my club down and through the ball. The impact of my club and the sand gives out a perfect *thump*, which is all I need to hear. It tells me I hit it just right, and I am completely at ease as my ball and the sand jump up onto the green. The ball takes one small hop toward the pin and stops dead. I have six feet straight uphill at the hole, and the crowd goes crazy. People are jumping up and down and clapping like mad. I can see the DJ off in the distance talking into his microphone, but the crowd noise is too loud to let me hear what he was saying. There is also now a TV crew from the local NBC affiliate covering the story. There has been TV coverage of the event in the past, but it wasn't anything like this. I step out of the bunker, wave to the sky like I am saying thank you to everyone for being there, and then rake the sand. I put my club in my golf bag, pull out my putter, and walk onto the green. Again, the sound of clapping is a welcome distraction.

I look around as I walk up to mark my ball, searching to see if Cindy is there by any chance. I told her about this tournament and asked her to come to the clubhouse afterwards to meet me for a drink. I want to introduce her to Max after the round. After all I put him through with Sammy ten years ago and Cindy today, he needs to see what these girls look like. I really don't expect her to be out here by the green. I told her to come later, thinking I wanted to get all the golf stuff out of the way and it would give us some time together with Max. Before today took the shape it did, my only expectations were to have a nice quiet dinner with the two of them. I had no idea there would be a fourth joining us in the form of Vanessa, but now that idea is a great thought. Still, I am hoping to spot her among all these people, but no such luck. I am excited about everything going on around me, and although Cindy and I haven't been romantically involved, I want to be with her more than anything in the world.

I hear this voice inside my head again, and it says plainly; *You'll see her in just a few. Finish the round. FINISH THE ROUND!*

Dustin is getting ready to putt. Since I am so close to the pin, I ask if he wants me to tend the pin. He nods yes. There is still about thirty feet left for him to negotiate his birdie putt. I stand to the right of the flag, watch his ball rolling towards me, pull the pin from the hole, and step back just a bit to not interfere with his ball. He has it on a great line and it looks like it has a chance. It starts slowing down sooner than I expect, and Dustin starts yelling, "Get going! GET GOING!" But despite his verbal passion, it runs out of speed less than a foot away. It is dead in the jar, but just stopped short. Everyone claps and he walks up to tap it in. He has played a good round of golf with the exception of a few really bad holes. I smile at Dustin and he just looks me dead in the eye and says, "Make it." I have grown to like this kid today and I know we'll be friends. I look forward to playing golf with him again outside of a tournament.

Max is next. I don't even offer him the pin. It's too close, and I know he won't want it. I set it down off to the side of the green and step out of the way, studying my line as I do. There is nothing in it. It's straight ahead, and I know all I have to do is not leave it short. There won't be any penalty being long, the crime will be having a putt to shoot 54 and leaving it short. I *know* I won't do that!

Max has a very makeable putt. He looks it over closely and stands up to the ball. The crowd is very respectful and nobody moves or makes a sound. I am amazed once again how quiet everyone can get. Max goes through his routine and is very methodical with his actions. I glance at Vanessa, who looks very nervous for her man, and I don't make eye contact with her. She is very obviously willing his putt in for him, and I don't want to break her focus. Max takes his stroke, and sure enough, he makes it to the roar of the crowd. He raises his putter over his head and smiles to the fans. He played great today, never once lost his temper, and shot a smooth 67, which will put him in second place all alone. I reach into the cup, pull out his ball, and toss it to him, grinning. He smiles back at me, then looks to Vanessa, who is absolutely glowing with pride.

I walk a few steps away to the coin marking the spot to replace my ball and put it just in front of the same coin I've used for many years, a 1954 Scottish Schilling. I found it at a thrift store the fall of my freshman year once Jack planted "54" in my head and since then, I haven't played a single round of golf without this treasured piece. Max sees I'm getting ready and he moves his hands up and down to quiet the crowd. I'm not at all concerned. I want them to continue to celebrate Max's putt. He deserves it, and I am extremely happy for him. I take my time walking around the putt from the other side of the cup and squatting down to make sure I'm not missing something in the break of the line, but it just confirms to me that it is dead straight. I am content. I know I can make this putt, and I don't allow my mind to go to the number, just stay in the moment. The words *"FINISH THE ROUND"* bounce again through my mind like an alarm set to do so every few minutes. One quick look from behind and I start in on it. I clear my mind of everything, but I can't do anything about the pounding of my heart. I take a few long breaths to try to keep it from jumping out of my chest. It is eerily quiet. I can't see anything but the line between my ball and the cup. I make my normal two short practice strokes, then put my putter behind the ball, rearrange my feet, look at the ball, look to the hole, back to my ball, and draw the club back and then forth with a smooth stroke. I refuse to look up to ensure I keep my head down and focus on the very back of the ball, where my putter has struck. I fully expect to hear the ball rattle in the cup, but I never do. Instead, I hear Max scream at the top of his lungs, "54!"

He knows it's in before it drops, and as I look up, the ball is gone. Max is just returning to earth from his leap. The sound of the crowd erupts. I straighten up as everyone moves toward me from every direction. I drop my putter and raise my hands over my head. Max grabs me and lifts me into the air before anyone else gets to me. Dustin grabs one leg and I am hoisted above the crowd that is now surrounding me. I feel like I just threw the last-second, winning touchdown in the Super Bowl! There has never been anything like this in my entire life. This feeling is better than anything I have ever imagined. I am laughing as people grab at me, shake my hand and give me high-fives. I look at Max, and Vanessa is holding him up. I catch her eye, she reaches her hand toward mine, I grab it and yell, "Vanessa!" at the same moment that she screams, "Jim!" But neither of us tries to say anything more over the noise. My hand is pulled in another direction and I watch her turn her attention to Max and plant a huge kiss on his face.

Joey is the one who has grabbed my arm. He is jumping up and down, all dignity forsaken, and yelling, "54! 54! 54!"

It is just an incredible moment, and I think that they are never going to put me down. I scan the crowd to take it all in. Behind the 18th green on the side of the clubhouse, I can see the starter's station. Right over it, there is the official clock to keep everyone on time, and I'll be damned if it didn't say 1:54! Colby is there in the crowd, reaching to give me a high-five. The kid is so cool, to be thirteen and out here competing is incredible. We lock eyes and he yells, "AWESOME!"

I look back over the crowd and out of the corner of my eye, I see four people standing on the hill just past the milling people. I immediately recognize Cindy, Wendy, Dan, and Liz! My heart jumps into my throat. I make eye contact with Cindy and she puts her hands over her mouth. I can see her eyes fill with tears, even at this distance. I reach my right hand toward her like I can pull her to me, but she is too far away. I pound Max on the shoulder to get his attention and yell, "Put me down!" He motions to Dustin and they set my feet back on the grass.

I can see Dan put his hand in the middle of Cindy's back and nudge her in my direction. I start pushing my way through the crowd, and she does the same from the other side as fast as she can with her slight limp. She is now reaching over people to try to get to me, and I grab her hand. Everyone realizes what's going on and moves aside. She throws her body against mine, tears running down her face, and presses her lips to mine as we embrace with all the passion built up over the last few months. Our mouths lock together and it is unbelievable. I keep kissing her and squeezing her closer to my body,

145

subconsciously attempting to make her as much a part of me as my own skin. People are clapping and cheering.

But we.

Just.

Keep.

Kissing.

Without breaking the contact of our lips, I start saying, "I love you, Cindy! I love you so much!"

Her tears drip down between our faces, salting our lips and adding to all the sensations. Cutting through the roaring of the crowd, and seeming louder than any of the cheers being uttered around us, I hear her sob, "I love you, Jim! I love you! I love you!"

## Acknowledgements

I would personally like to thank the following for their help making this book possible. First and foremost, my wife Tracy who is my best friend and my partner in everything I do. My son Oliver who was more of an inspiration for this book than anyone and we spent an enormous amount of time discussing this story. Oliver has also designed and is the artist for the front cover of this book, thank you Oliver! My daughter Chloe who at age 10 read the PG version of this book to me word for word after the first draft and her enthusiasm was truly encouraging. My parents Barbara and Ben for their constant love and support. My brothers Steven and David for being there my entire life. I couldn't have completed this book without the help of Cassidy Paige Warner, the dedication and writing expertise she brought to this project will forever be appreciated. The following people had a tremendous amount of input on "54": Gina and Ted Oldenburg, Dr. Norman Rice, Mark Miller, Stacy Schroeder, Paul Peck, Reade Bailey, Richard Carnes, Skip Guss, Gary McCord, Susan Pesso, Joe Kamby, Bill Wilto, Sam Kuller and Michael Mumford. A special thank you goes to Kelly and David Leadbetter for their friendship and inspiration over the years!

"May all your days be filled with Birdies!"